World Art
in the
Berlin Museums

World Art
in the
Berlin Museums

National Gallery Berlin
Staatliche Museen
Preußischer Kulturbesitz

Authors of the captions to the plates:

Matthias Eberle	ME
Lucius Grisebach	LG
Dieter Honisch	DH
Peter Krieger	PK
Michael Pauseback	MP
Angela Schneider	AS

English translation: J. W. Gabriel, Berlin

Photographic credits:

All color plates:
Photoatelier Jörg P. Anders, Berlin
Black and white illustrations
1–3, 5: National Gallery Archive
4, 6: Reinhard Friedrich, Berlin

Cover design:

Christian Ahlers

© 1980 by Belser AG
für Verlagsgeschäfte & Co. KG,
Stuttgart und Zürich
Address: Belser Verlag,
Falkertstraße 73, D-7000 Stuttgart 1
© 1980 by Cosmopress, Genf, for Salvador Dali,
Paul Klee, Oskar Kokoschka, Serge Poliakoff,
Karl Schmidt-Rottluff.
© 1980 by SPADEM, Paris/BILD-KUNST,
Bonn, for Max Ernst, Fernand Léger, Claude
Monet, Pierre Auguste Renoir, Wols.
© 1980 by BILD-KUNST, Bonn, for
Max Beckmann.
© 1980 by Estate of George Grosz, Princeton, N.J.
© 1980 by. S.I.A.E., Rom/BILD-KUNST,
Bonn, for Giorgio de Chirico.
© 1980 by Dr. Wolfgang and Ingeborg Henze,
Campione d'Italia, for Ernst Ludwig Kirchner.
All rights reserved
Produced by Druckhaus Tempelhof, Berlin
Printed on 120 g/sq.m. all-rag white 'Ikonofix'
made by Zanders Paper Co., Bergisch-Gladbach
Printed in Germany
ISBN 3-7630-2027-6

Preface

"The purpose of a museum is clearly to further art, to spread taste in art and to provide for its enjoyment. It is quite naturally to the great, conspicuous works that our feeling first turns and by which it may test itself, free of all pedantry or even the need for profound study." Thus Wilhelm von Humboldt, writing to his monarch, explained his support for the first public museum established in Prussia. *Das Alte Museum,* the architect Friedrich Schinkel's most famous building, was opened on August 3, 1830. Since that date the Royal, then Prussian State Museums, which after World War II continued in the western sector of Berlin under the aegis of a foundation, the *Stiftung Preussischer Kulturbesitz,* have developed into institutions of international rank.

These fourteen museums and affiliated institutes devoted to research in the natural and museum sciences were and still are an organization unique in the world. Many collections of higher quality, and certainly larger ones, exist, but there is no second museum complex that was planned from the outset as "a public, well-chosen art collection," as Frederick Wilhelm III put it in 1810, rather than starting as a royal painting gallery, a collection of classical antiquities, ethnographic cabinet or museum of arts and crafts. World art and world culture have found a home in the Berlin Museums.

More clearly than any other great German museum, the history of the Prussian collections in Berlin reflects our nation's fateful history over the past century and a half. Founded as Royal Prussian Museums, they served, clandestinely if you will, as national museums during the Empire, Weimar Republic and through the end of World War II. Finally, when Germany was divided, they stood in the west for a new beginning and reconstruction, under a Foundation supported by Berlin, Bonn and the Western German states, while in the other half of the former capital they became East German government institutions.

Long before 1830 the founders had begun to collect systematically, led by aims not only of an artistic but of a scholarly and educational nature. Masterpieces of world art, they reasoned, made available to every citizen and recorded and published in collection catalogues, would further the humanistic ideals they were devoted to. From the beginning, scholarship and dissemination of knowledge were given equal weight.

These ideals have lost none of their importance during the one hundred and fifty years since the founding of the first public museum in Prussia. Hence it is incumbent on the State Museums, particularly in this Jubilee Year, to give an account of themselves, taking their tradition as a challenge. This series of guides was prepared to that end. The present booklet is part of the series, just as the museum it introduces is an independent part of the *Preussischer Kulturbesitz* Foundation.

Stephan Waetzoldt
Director General
Stiftung Preussischer Kulturbesitz

Introduction

In view of the German situation, the name *Nationalgalerie* may well seem anachronistic. It goes back far into the nineteenth century, and those who conceived it did so out of a desire to unify, if only in name, many diversities. The idea of a national culture is rooted in the thinking of the Romantic Period; the notion of devoting a museum to this idea dates back to 1848, when a group of Düsseldorf artists raised the demand for an institution to further contemporary art. Their hope was realized in 1861 with a bequest to the King of Prussia made by J. H. W. Wagener, a Berlin businessman and Royal Swedish Consul. Wegener's collection comprised two hundred and sixty-two works, mostly German but also by artists of other European countries, and besides many lesser works it included paintings by Karl Friedrich Schinkel and Caspar David Friedrich. Thus the core of the Berlin collection, rather than depending on royal or noble patronage, was shaped by a combination of artists' initiative and private collector's commitment. These factors have been constants in the museum's history down to the present day.

The *Nationalgalerie's* first home, a building designed by August Stühler under the neo-classical influence of Schinkel, was begun in 1866, in the centre of the arts and sciences complex on Museum Island. Construction was held up by the Franco-Prussian War, and the building was not finished until 1876. This latter-day Greek temple on its high base might have been an imposing Hall of Fame, but as a contemporary museum it had its drawbacks. The rooms were too lofty, the lighting insufficient; and as their collections grew, curators were faced with the necessity of making improvements. They were also obligated by the inscription on the pediment, *To German Art*, to a task that was difficult even for men of goodwill. All purchases were subject to the vote of a commission which the State of Prussia installed to oversee artistic matters, and its decisions tended to the parochial.

The first Chief Curator, the gifted scholar Max Jordan (1876−1896), was able to overcome these limitations only partially. He did however put the museum's work on a scholarly basis, build up an indispensable reference library, arrange for a travel budget, and invest great effort not only in improving the collection but in systematically cataloguing it. Though he lamented the dearth of foreign art in the collection, Jordan did not quite succeed in separating the categories of partiotic show and aesthetic worth. In this he was no more than typical of his era.

Upon Jordan's demission, Hugo von Tschudi (1896−1909), long a collaborator of Wilhelm von Bode, was named Curator of the *Nationalgalerie,* which had been newly incorporated into the Royal Museum group. Von Tschudi was a scholar and a gentleman who came of a good Swiss family, but at the time still more promising than experienced. Such key museum men as Alfred Lichtwark in Hamburg let their scepticism be known. But von Tschudi surprised everyone with his daring approach, and the reactions bordered on violence. Prepared by the ideas of the Marées-Fiedler circle in Rome of which he was part, and encouraged by Max Liebermann, he was very quick to realize the European significance of the Impressionists. Government moneys not being available to buy them, he accepted donations from bankers, most of them Jewish, of paintings by Manet, Monet, Renoir and Cézanne. The vanguard art of Germany's old political rival thus found its way into the *Nationalgalerie* before French museums had begun to consider it. And official Germany was infuriated. A Royal Cabinet Order was issued

1. The National Gallery on Museum Island

requiring all acquisitions, including gifts, to be authorized, a measure that was to cripple the museum for twenty years to come. This did not daunt von Tschudi, however. In the thirteen years of office before his opponents forced his early resignation, he transformed a congeries of patriotic sculptures and paintings into a truly national collection that compared favourably with any in Europe. The standards von Tschudi set have remained valid to this day.

His successor, Ludwig Justi (1909–1933), replied to conflict with administrative reform, detaching the collection from the Museum Group, reconstituting the Purchasing Commission – which raised Max Liebermann's ire – and finally separating the old collection, which remained in the original building, from new acquisitions. These, installed in 1919 at the *Kronprinzenpalais,* Unter den Linden, together with exhibitions and educational programmes, were to

make Justi's *Nationalgalerie* the leading museum of modern art in Europe. If von Tschudi had opened the museum's doors to the Impressionists, Marées and Böcklin, Justi reopened them to the Expressionists, Munch and van Gogh. Yet as his success grew, so did the number of his enemies. By the late 1920s conservative art critics had managed to set off a vituperous campaign against the *Kronprinzenpalais* and modern art in general which eventually led to Justi's dismissal by the National Socialists in 1933.

Their propaganda exhibition, *Degenerate Art,* which Justi's successor, Eberhard Hanfstaengl (1933–1937) tried in vain to prevent, destroyed the life's work of a courageous and farsighted man. Four hundred and thirty-five works of art were confiscated, sold off for a pittance and scattered around the world; such invaluable paintings as Franz Marc's *Tower of Blue Horses* were never seen again.

8

2. The *Kronprinzenpalais,* Unter den Linden

In 1939 the premises of the *Nationalgalerie* were closed. Paul Ortwin Rave, who was later to hold the office of Chief Curator (1945–1950), supervised removal and provisional storage of the collection and finally its installment in special depots at Wiesbaden and Celle. Its return to Berlin had to wait until 1953 to 1957; but by that time the *Nationalgalerie* had been bisected into western and eastern administrations – the year was 1948.

During its exile the Magistrate of Greater Berlin under Adolf Jannasch had already commemorated the *Kronprinzenpalais* by establishing, in 1945, the *Galerie des 20. Jahrhunderts.* Its collection, an attempt to carry on the museum's traditions, grew rapidly and in 1954 was opened to the public in a building on Jebenstrasse.

Leopold Reidemeister was in 1957 named Director General of the State Museums remaining in the western sector of Berlin and also Chief Curator of the *Nationalgalerie.* He opened its re-established collection in 1959, at the *Grosse Orangerie,* Charlottenburg Palace. And he, too, attempted to fill the gaps torn by war and Nazism by purchases of contemporary art, an enterprise whose success demanded all the powers he could marshal.

It was a propitious decision to combine the two collections in a new building, which by now had become imperative. Designed by Ludwig Mies van der Rohe, last president of the Bauhaus, which had been closed in Berlin in 1933, the *Neue Nationalgalerie* was headed from 1967 to 1974 by Werner Haftmann. He circumspectly fused the two collections and, through his compelling words and acts, again brought the museum to international awareness.

Our task today is to guide the collection firmly into the contemporary stream, to link its newer acquisitions with the older

9

3. The New National Gallery, near the Tiergarten

4. View of the exhibition *New York in Europe. American Art in European Collections,* 1976. Sculpture by Tony Smith and a painting by Morris Louis

5. View of the Kenneth Snelson exhibition, 1977

6. View of the Panamarenko exhibition, 1978

works by painstaking purchase of the classic moderns, and to revive the private initiative which had been so crucial during earlier periods of the museum's history. The *Freunde der Nationalgalerie,* a group of supporters founded in 1929 by Ludwig Justi and dispersed in 1937 by the Nazi authorities, was re-established in 1977. In the meantime this group has not only celebrated its fiftieth anniversary but can boast a membership of 500. Thanks to a number of major acquisitions, its name is indissolubly linked with the *Nationalgalerie.*

Over 300,000 people visit the museum annually, attracted by its collection but also by its special events, which in addition to temporary exhibitions include concerts, theatre performances, guided tours and festive entertainments.

I hope this small guide will serve to point you the way to fifty-three of the finest works in our collection, facilitate your understanding of them, refresh your memory and perhaps even encourage you to make a second visit. My thanks go to all of my colleagues who assisted in its preparation and wrote the captions to the plates.

DH

Colour plates

1 Gottlieb Schick (1776–1812)

Portrait of Heinrike Dannecker (1773–1823), 1802.
Oil on canvas, 119 × 100 cm.

This imposing portrait of Heinrike Dannecker was painted in Stuttgart in 1802. Silhouetted against the sky far above the distant horizon, she looks out at us candidly with a graceful turn of the head. The red, white and blue of her fashionable costume recall – certainly not by chance – the colours of the French flag, and against the deep blue of the skirt glow the delicate hues of her bouquet of bluebells, a rose, buttercups and clover.

Mrs. Dannecker, a former Miss Rapp, was the first wife of the sculptor J. H. Dannecker, Schick's friend and teacher. It was from him that Schick learned to model forms so boldly, but also to capture the expression of a face with such compelling naturalness as he has here. Dannecker's house on Schlossplatz with its collections of casts from Greek and Roman sculpture was a favorite Stuttgart meeting place for friends of the arts. Mrs. Dannecker's pose – elbow resting on her knee, hand at her chin, and crossed legs – can be traced via her husband's own sculpture back to antiquity, where variations of it are found both in free-standing figures and sarcophagus reliefs. But Schick's debt to Greek and Roman art, ideal and highest standard of the Neo-classical age to which this portrait belongs, comes out in other respects as well. His portrayal of the whole-length figure in profile, rare in portraiture, with the head turned out of the plane, gives his painting almost the look of a relief, an impression which is further increased by his incisive tracing of the elegantly curving contours. And the stone bench Mrs. Dannecker is seated on certainly recalls a fragment from some Greek or Roman ruin.

Schick had spent three years working in the Paris studio of Jacques-Louis David, the famous Neo-classical artist, an experience which did much to prepare him for this fine achievement. *Heinrike Dannecker* immediately put him in the first rank of German portrait painters, at the age of twenty-six.

PK

2 Friedrich Overbeck (1789—1869)

The Painter Franz Pforr (1788–1812), c. 1810–12.
Oil on canvas, 62 × 47 cm.

In 1808, a group of young artists in Vienna came together to found the *Lukasbund,* a league whose romantic aim was to revive Christian art and Christian subject-matter and whose ideal was the Middle Ages. Two years later they went to Rome, where they moved into an abandoned monastery – and where their long hair quickly earned them the nickname "Nazarenes", by which they are still known. Friedrich Overbeck and Franz Pforr, the artist and his sitter, were the leaders of this group and they also formulated the principles that guided its work. The portrait one did of the other is a superb example of the Nazarene style.

Close friends who were involved in a continual exchange of ideas, Overbeck and Pforr expressed through their paintings both the role they assigned to themselves in contemporary art and their relationship to art of the past, and Pforr even put their aims in literary form by writing a short novel. They saw themselves as rejuvenating the two great European traditions, Overbeck that of Italian art and Pforr that of medieval German art. To embody these traditions they invented what they called "ideal brides", a dark-haired maiden by the name of Italia or Sulamith and a blonde Germania or Maria. Here, Overbeck has portrayed his friend against the background of this modern mythology.

In terms of composition, this portrait of a half-length figure in a rounded arch with window parapet belongs to fifteenth-century Netherlandish and Italian tradition, and Pforr's costume, known as a German coat, was adopted by the Nazarenes from medieval attire. In the Gothic room in the background, Overbeck has evoked the domestic peace which he desired for his friend – a blonde and gentle bride, knitting and reading a religious book in an attitude that recalls the Virgin Mary in many portrayals of the Annunciation. This similarity is borne out by the stalk of while lilies on the table next to her, a medieval symbol for the Virgin.

This depiction of an ideal homelife has many overtones of a religious and historic kind, to which the cat rubbing up against Pforr's arm on the window ledge adds a note of earthly domesticity. The old German city with its Gothic church and the landscape in the medieval manner in the background, stand for the tradition in which Pforr's art found sustenance.

LG

3 Josef Anton Koch (1768–1839)

The Falls at Subiaco, 1813.
Oil on canvas, 58 × 68 cm.

Born into a Tyrolese peasant family, Josef Anton Koch was lucky enough to find patrons who enabled him to attend the renowned *Karlsschule* in Stuttgart. This was the school where only a few years before Friedrich Schiller had written *Die Räuber* – and whose strict discipline he had fled shortly thereafter. Koch did the same. After escaping to France, where he joined up with the Jacobins for a time until their goings-on became too much for him, he set off on foot for Switzerland and Italy, finally settling in Rome in 1795.

Rome, that great repository of art, was not only an education in itself for Koch; like many other German artists of the period, it reminded him of a glorious past, the promise of a Golden Age which still seemed to live on in the city and its environs. On long walking tours through the nearby hills in the vicinity of Subiaco he filled an entire sketchbook with drawings, "among which are many," he wrote, "that particularly if I help them along a bit, will do as compositions, and especially if I mix some story or other into them". This combination of landscape and historic narrative became such a speciality of Koch's that it made him the founder of an entire school, that of the heroic or historical landscape so popular in the nineteenth century.

As the French armies approached in 1812, he fled to Vienna, where he painted *The Falls at Subiaco*. It is a picture that shows more than can be taken in at one glance. Everything, even background details, is in perfect focus, drawing the eye into the scene. We are invited to explore an ideal landscape meant to satisfy both the emotions, by communicating a sense of liberty, and the mind, by providing an image of nature perfected.

The terrain is composed of three distinct types – a valley out of which foothills rise to a high mountain chain. Each zone represents a typical aspect of the Italian countryside with its precisely observed details; together they stand for nature as a whole, including man and his works. Each has its characteristic vegetation, and to each has been assigned the human activity performed there since time began: farming in the valley, shepherding in the hills, and hunting in the mountains. It is an image of nature inhabited, even to the cliffs where a column of smoke rises, by humble labouring people whose mode of life has remained unchanged for centuries.

Koch's aim was to stimulate thought, to transport the spectator, as he wrote, "into other ages, imaginative worlds" with his visions of man and nature in timeless harmony. When he composed his Italian sketches into this painting at his Vienna studio, it was out of a longing he shared with many of his contemporaries – the longing for a simple life, lived in freedom.   ME

4 Caspar David Friedrich (1774—1840)

The Solitary Tree (Village Landscape in Morning Light), 1822.
Oil on canvas, 55 × 71 cm.

In this painting and that on the following page, both done in 1822 for the Berlin collector, Consul Wagener, Friedrich illustrated two quite different reactions to nature. Dissatisfied with conventional types of landscape painting – Koch's historic landscapes were anathema to him – he emphasized over and over again that artists could develop a true conception of nature only by looking at what "that most ancient of all masters" had put before them.

What Friedrich looked for were signs in nature that would reveal its divine origin and that could provide clues to mankind's destiny. This search was obviously a result of his deeply religious upbringing, but it also reflected a widespread hope of his age, the period of the French occupation and subsequent Restoration – the hope that nature could be a source of enlightenment and guarantor of a better future.

The first painting depicts a broad, sparsely inhabited plain with mountains rising in the background and an old oak tree towering above a pond in the foreground. A shepherd leans against its trunk, he and his flock probably meant to symbolize an age long past when man still lived in harmony with his surroundings. The earliest forms of human settlement appear further back, a village built around an old abandoned monastery in a wood, these apparently meant to stand for the Middle Ages. Still further back, a city lies concealed in a deeper valley. Mountains overtop the scene, their peaks mingling with the clouds. To the thinking of the day – Kant and Schiller are two prime examples – mountains and the seacoast were places where human beings, made aware of their insignificance and weakness, were compelled to turn to ideas, to reflect on the future and on the meaning of their lives.

Now if the oak tree is taken to symbolize mankind – or the German people – then it grew and flourished in times long past, times in which it was still a landmark, a sign of support and orientation. The same is true of the primordial life it shelters and which many other artists besides Friedrich portrayed. The tree's crown still extends into the sky, pointing towards the future; but it has been blasted by lightning, and can clearly no longer serve as a sign of hope. ME

20

5 Caspar David Friedrich (1774−1840)

Moonrise over the Sea, 1822.
Oil on canvas, 55 × 71 cm.

In the second painting commissioned by Wagener, Friedrich suggests a way out of the dilemma posed in *The Solitary Tree*. It shows three people, two women and a man, watching the moon rise over the sea from a rock on a lonely beach. The light of day is gone, but the moon brings new light into the darkness; Friedrich himself once remarked in jest that when he died, his soul would certainly go to the moon.

Two ships are approaching the shore across the moonlit sea, heading directly towards the figures. Now a ship, of course, is a very ancient symbol of man, tossed by the storms of life and in search of a safe harbour. Here, the human beings themselves apparently represent that harbour, and the ships' approach is a sign to them of where they must look for the message that is to raise them above their transitory, earthbound existence − in themselves, by reflecting on their desolate situation in view of the natural phenomena that point beyond it. The solution is to be found, Friedrich seems to say, only in subjective contemplation of nature and not in old traditional symbols.

That his figures' thoughts may well be not only religious but political in nature, is shown by the medieval German costume the man is wearing. It was the costume of an opposition group called the Demagogues, who suffered particularly under the prevailing conditions because their high hopes for a united, liberal and democratic Germany following the 1813−15 War of Liberation had come to nothing.   ME

6 Karl Friedrich Schinkel (1781—1841)

Banks of the Spree near Stralau, 1817.
Oil on canvas, 36 × 44.5 cm.

Schinkel, though best known for his neo-classical architecture in Prussia, was a universal talent whose paintings put him in the first rank of German Romantic artists. The Schinkel Museum with the artist's bequest was up to the last war part of the Nationalgalerie, which today still possesses the majority of his surviving works in oil.

Schinkel's style was strongly influenced by the work of Caspar David Friedrich, and, like him, his subject was landscape symbolic of human ideas and emotions. Yet unlike Friedrich, Schinkel always brought buildings into his scenes, man-made works which spoke the same language as nature. One such architectural landscape, a depiction of a Gothic church in a forest, he inscribed thus: "An attempt to express the tender longing melancholy which fills the heart at the sound of a service echoing across from a church."

Banks of the Spree near Stralau is a river landscape typical of the Brandenburg plains but fit out with dramatic figures and given the sublimity of a classical Mediterranean scene. The two horn-players in their skiff, framed by a Renaissance arch, would be equally at home in the Blue Grotto of Capri. Despite its title, this is no realistic portrayal of a definite locale on the River Spree but a mixture of actual and imagined motifs. The skyline of Berlin is visible on the horizon as it actually looked at the time, with French and German cathedrals and the Theatre on Gendarmenmarkt. The buildings in the right centre and the trees silhouetted against the sunset, however, are pure inventions. To further increase the drama of the scene, Schinkel has framed it entire in the arch of a bridge. In an earlier version of the same motif (lost during the Second World War), the view appeared with a different foreground. The boat was different in shape and the arch had a trellis attached to it which was overgrown with grapevines.

LG

7 Eduard Gaertner (1801–1877)

Parochialstrasse (formerly Reetzengasse), 1831.
Oil on canvas, 39 × 29 cm.

Parochialstrasse was one of those typical narrow streets in the old quarter of Berlin near the Royal Palace, an area which has since been destroyed without a trace. Only their names are left, and the paintings that Eduard Gaertner did from 1830 to 1870. Gaertner specialized in architectural views, which had been an independent genre since the seventeenth century. Down through the nineteenth century, to that period known in Germany as Biedermeier, most European cities had artists who devoted themselves wholly to recording the architectural aspect of their town. In Berlin, this was Gaertner, whose success took him temporarily to Moscow and St. Petersburg as well.

Though he preferred to depict Berlin's more impressive avenues and official buildings (see *Die Neue Wache*, 1833, and *Unter den Linden*, 1853, both in the Nationalgalerie), Gaertner never painted pompous "portraits" of edifices but lively street scenes from the pedestrian's point of view. In his paintings of the old quarter (see also his *Klosterstrasse*, 1830, and *Brüderstrasse*, 1863), such landmarks are visible only in glimpses, like the tower of Nikolaikirche in the background haze here. The street is lined with small, three- and four-storey houses, most of them probably eighteenth century, unassuming middle-class residences typical of the period. The inhabitants are going about their everyday business, and nothing particularly dramatic occurs; Gaertner has kept the figures small in scale, like accessories to the scene.

This points to an essential characteristic of the painting, namely that everything in it has been treated as of equal importance. With that certain sobriety of view which nowadays is often termed "photographic", the artist has seen and recorded everything with the same degree of attention – the cobblestone paving, water in the gutter, human figures, light glancing on the facades. The painting's subject is one particular, very individual street as a living whole, a place apart from the rest of the city that exudes security and comfort and possesses an atmosphere as personal as a country village.

LG

8 Karl Blechen (1798—1840)

Interior of the Palm House, 1832.
Oil on paper mounted on canvas, 64 × 56 cm.

Though Karl Blechen was one of the most remarkable talents in nineteenth-century Germany, the Berlin artist's achievement has yet to be recognized in its true light and appraised within the context of European art. One reason for this neglect is surely the fact that his works have remained concentrated in a few places and hardly ever shown outside Berlin.

With rare clarity, Blechen's art embodies the transition from late Romanticism to a new and objective realism based on the phenomena of light and colour. A late-comer to art, his meeting in Dresden with the Norwegian landscape painter, Johan Christian Clausen Dahl — and possibly also with Dahl's friend, Caspar David Friedrich – did much to point him the way. But the really decisive event in his life was his journey to Italy, which in 1828—29 took him from the Alps down to Capri and Paestum. What fascinated him there were less the archaeology and history of the country than the brilliant sunlight that flooded everything, ruins and cities and countryside alike.

Working from the store of sketches and watercolours he had brought back with him from the South – nearly a thousand in all – Blechen began a series of larger compositions. Though these did not always retain the freshness and spontaneity of his first attempts, they nevertheless proved too unconventional for Berlin audiences, who had different ideas about what Italy must look like. It was not until 1832 that Blechen received what was to remain his most important commission, when Friedrich Wilhelm III asked him for two paintings of the new Palm House on Peacock Island as a gift for his daughter, Charlotte, Czarina of Russia.

The Palm House was built in 1830 to house a collection of exotic plants which the king had purchased in Paris. Its architect, Schinkel, heightened the Indian look of the cast-iron building by employing fragments of Burmese architecture, and in his painting, Blechen has dramatized this oriental aspect by adding reclining odalisques. The space is suffused by sunlight filtering down from the high glazed roof and creating a richly nuanced play of warm green tones. The building no longer exists, having been destroyed by fire in 1880.   PK

9 Karl Spitzweg (1808–1885)

The Poor Poet, 1839.
Oil on canvas, 36,3 × 44,7 cm.

Spitzweg's *Poor Poet*, one of the most popular of all nineteenth-century German paintings, was also the first of which he executed two, almost identical versions in rapid succession. Ours is the second version, of 1839; the first, done in 1837, now hangs in the Neue Pinakothek in Munich. When Spitzweg exhibited this first version at the 1839 show of the Munich Art Society, he harvested nothing but derision.

Spitzweg's poet lies on a mattress in the corner of his bare garret, kept warm by a ragged robe, a nightcap and an old blanket. An umbrella fastened to the ceiling protects him from the leaky roof. His bed is ensconced in books; his coat, boots and walking stick await his pleasure around the stove. The workaday world and the cold, sunny winter weather remain banned outside his window. His quill between his teeth, he is engrossed in marking the rhythm of a verse which he has apparently just written; a classical Greek hexameter on the wall serves to remind him of his ideal. Yet his efforts seem not to have come to much, for he has been using the products of his art to heat his stove – the bundles of paper in front of it bear the Latin titles *opera meorum fasc. III* and *IV*, or *Volumes III and IV of My Own Works*. The first two volumes seem to have gone up in smoke already.

With this memorable figure of a literary man who has lost all touch with the outside world and sees his salvation in a revival of classic, academic verse, Spitzweg poked devastating fun at the exaggerated importance his contemporaries placed on the art of poetry. The 1830s still fed off the great classical renascence which Goethe und Schiller and others had brought about and which made literature the leading art in Germany. Their imitators had long taken over the field, however, and it was their hollowness, their diehard adherence to classical ideals, which Spitzweg personified here.

LG

10 John Constable (1776−1837)

The Admiral's House in Hampstead, or
"The Grove", 1821−22.
Oil on canvas, 60 × 50 cm.

In the early nineteenth century, Hampstead was still a quiet farming and trading village outside London and anything but an artists' colony. Constable moved into a house there in 1821, and over the following years, besides four large canvases the most famous of which, *Hay Cart*, caused a great sensation at the 1824 Paris Salon, he painted a number of intimate views of the town. Among them were three versions of the Admiral's House. One of these, an oil sketch at the Victoria and Albert Museum in London, may possibly be a study for the painting in our collection. The view, as John Baskett has shown, is that which Constable must have had from the top storey of his residence at 2, Lower Terrace.

We look down on a path with a few passersby and windblown trees; further back, behind two smaller buildings, rises the Admiral's House, a squarish edifice that at the time was still known as "The Grove". It was built for Admiral Matthew Burton (1715−1795) who had the roof fitted out like a ship's quarterdeck and used to fire off cannon shots from it on appropriate occasions. A grove of trees, a tall poplar and a threatening sky complete the scene.

Despite its solid internal composition based on the accentuated verticals of the buildings, the view Constable has chosen has an everyday, almost accidental look, like a snapshot. This effect is primarily one of lighting, and it is underscored by the impetuous brushwork. Foliage and walls glisten in the sun, which has apparently just broken through the clouds between rainshowers somewhere off to the right. Constable had long been fascinated by this kind of atmospheric effect, and, especially during his Hampstead years, he made countless studies of cloud formations, adding precise meteorological commentary. His aim was to depict nature − portraits and historical painting did not interest him − as unpretentiously and straightforwardly as he knew how, without allegorical or mythological trimming. This departure from tradition, together with a vision out to capture optical sensations which led to his relaxed, free style, assured Constable's work of a great influence on the Barbizon School of landscape painters, as well as on the young Menzel. Yet it was not until half a century later, with early Impressionism, that this approach found wide acceptance.   AS

11 Carl Rottmann (1797–1850)

Battlefield at Marathon, c. 1849.
Oil on canvas, 91 × 90.5 cm.

In 1826 Rottmann, who had come to Munich five years earlier, was commissioned by Ludwig I of Bavaria to paint twenty-eight views of Italy for the arcades of the Royal Residence there. This "Journey to Italy in Pictures" finished, he received a second large commission, in 1833, for a series of landscapes which was to encompass thirty-eight historic sites in Greece. This ambitious project probably owed its inception to the coronation of Ludwig's son, Otto I, as King of Greece in 1832, an honour which he in turn owed largely to his father's enthusiasm for that country.

Rottmann spent the year of 1834–35 touring the Peleponnesus and neighbouring islands at Ludwig's expense. The Greece he found, crushed and impoverished by the wars of independence against the Turks, was a far cry from the classical Greece of Winckelmann, on whose ideals he had been raised; nevertheless, the countryside and brilliant Mediterranean sky could not help but inspire him.

Back in Bavaria, Rottmann began to work up the many sketches and watercolours he had made on site. Like the Italian views, the new series of oils was planned for installation in the royal garden arcades. But from 1839 to his death in 1850, Rottmann was able to complete only twenty-four of the projected thirty-eight paintings. They were exhibited in 1854 at the recently opened Neue Pinakothek, in a room designed especially to house them.

The painting illustrated here was probably finished in 1849, the same year as, if not slightly later than the *Marathon* of the Munich cycle, from which it differs in important respects. The historic event itself – the Battle of Marathon at which the Greeks vanquished the Persian armies in 490 B. C., thus laying the groundwork for western civilization – is not depicted here at all. Spread out before us is a deserted, seemingly uninhabitable expanse, and above the red earth – it recalls the carnage that took place here – a vast primeval sky arches, darkened by storm clouds through which the sun breaks in places, illuminating patches of the plain and sea. Sky and earth, sea and clouds, rather than being sharply defined, merge into a unity, a cosmic image of nature determined, like the primordial state itself, by genesis and decline.

AS

12 Adolph von Menzel (1815—1905)

The Balcony Room, 1845.
Oil on cardboard, 58 × 47 cm.

In addition to the history paintings which brought him fame during his lifetime, Menzel did many studies of a much more intimate kind, like his beautiful *Balcony Room*. Mostly of interiors or views from the windows of his apartments, these paintings did not become known until shortly before Menzel's death, since as mere studies he considered them too personal for public exhibition.

Pictured here is the living room in Menzel's residence at 18, Schöneberger Strasse, where he and his mother lived in 1845 before moving to 43, Ritterstrasse in what today is the Kreuzberg district of Berlin (see his *Bedroom*, done there in 1847). The view is of a corner of the room with a tall mirror and two chairs at the right, and at the left, the arm of a sofa with a carpet before it. The balcony door is open; a gentle breeze billows the white lace curtain. The mood is that of a comfortable apartment on a summer day. The bright sunlight, subdued by the curtain, plays across the floor. One senses how cool the room must be compared to the heat outside.

The painting has remained unfinished. Though the sofa is clearly reflected in the mirror, it is visible at the left only as a contoured area of underpainting; and the picture on the wall above it likewise appears only in the mirror. Menzel has signed and dated the work, however, which indicates that he must have considered its present state final.

Unlike the official history painting of the day with its sublime and heroic themes, this private work of Menzel's had no other purpose than to capture a momentary glimpse of beauty, to translate a fluttering curtain and glancing sunlight into pure painting. Here, Menzel achieved in his personal realm something which only much later was advocated and defended in public – by the Impressionists – and which Max Liebermann once summed up in a famous phrase: "A nicely painted head of cabbage is better than a badly painted Virgin."

For Menzel, this picture meant practice in achieving an equal vividness of handling in his official commissions (his *Flute Concert*, for example). A contemporary observer may well find its frankness of approach more to his taste than the finish and pomp of the artist's historical canvases.

LG

13 Adolph von Menzel (1815–1905)

The Flute Concert, 1852.
Oil on canvas, 142 × 205 cm.

By the time he had completed the illustrations for Franz Kugler's opus, *History of Frederick the Great,* Menzel had become an expert on the Prussian king and his milieu. In 1850 he began a series of eight paintings on Frederick's life, the best of which are now considered to be *Dinner at Sanssouci* (1850, destroyed in the war) and *The Flute Concert* (1852). Neither showed the king in his public role as statesman but among his closer circle, devoting himself to the pursuit of philosophy and music.

The setting here is the Concert Hall of Sanssouci Palace near Potsdam, on an evening in the year 1750. Frederick stands in the centre of the room, about to begin the concert, as the orchestra awaits its cue and the guests listen expectantly. We know who Menzel included in his reconstruction of the scene because he entered their names on one of his drawings. Most of them were members of the king's personal retinue: standing at the left, Freiherr Jakob Friedrich von Bielefeld, Count Gustav Adolf von Gotter, and Pierre de Maupertius, President of the Academy of Science; seated, Frederick's sister, Princess Amalie, with her lady-in-waiting, and behind them, Choirmaster Graun; in the centre of the picture, seated beneath the chandelier, Frederick's favourite sister, Margravine Wilhelmine von Brandenburg-Bayreuth, whose visit had been the occasion of the concert, and behind the king to the right, Sophie Caroline, Countess of Camas; behind her stands the Chevalier Chasot. Seated at the harpsichord is Philipp Emanuel Bach, Johann Sebastian's son, and standing in the orchestra, viola at the ready, is Franz Benda, the concert master. Johann Joachim Quandt, Frederick's flute teacher, listens intently at the right.

Menzel's aim was to reconstruct the historic moment down to every detail, no matter how seemingly insignificant. To this end he studied the personalities and their costumes, and the furnishings and decor of the room, in hundreds of exhaustive drawings. But besides historical accuracy, he wanted to transmit the atmosphere of the event – "candlelight from all sides and from above," as he wrote – and thus to rescue it from the past, filling the scene with human warmth and immediate presence.

LG

14 Anselm Feuerbach (1829—1880)

Ricordo di Tivoli, 1866—67.
Oil on canvas, 194 × 131 cm.

Of all that group of artists known as the Germans in Rome, Feuerbach had perhaps the finest sensibility. Though the mood of his work was located somewhere between Böcklin's dramatic inventiveness and Marées' classical calm, it came even closer to his great Italian Renaissance models, above all to Raphael and Titian. If his early paintings of Nanna, the dear companion who left him in 1865, had much of the spiritual serenity of Titian, his later portrayals of Iphigenia and Medea were marked by a pathos all the more dramatic for its being forcefully contained.

The painting in our collection was done in Rome, and the artist mentioned it in a letter to his mother in 1866, remarking that it was an "oddly happy" composition. Indeed it has a quiet and relaxed composure, that "Raphaelesque touch" of which he later spoke. Beyond the boy and girl absorbed in their music, the waterfalls of Tivoli are visible, lending the image a unity of figure and landscape, narrative and form, rare in Feuerbach's work, and making it a superb evocation of natural innocence. The artist has largely succeeded here in overcoming the strictures of subject-matter and form to develop a unique pictorial language which imbues the very traditional subject with modern sensibility.

This painting, like Marées' *The Golden Age* (see No. 16), was once part of the collection of Konrad Fiedler, who like Count Schack before him furthered both artists and wrote about their work. It was purchased for the Nationalgalerie in 1902 by its director, Hugo von Tschudi, who as a young man had frequented the Germans in Rome circle.   DH

15 Hans von Marées (1837—1887)

The Rowers, 1873.
Oil on canvas, 136 × 167 cm.

The Rowers is an oil study for the main fresco at the Zoological Station established in Naples by Anton Dohrn in 1872, a republic of science where scholars of many countries gathered to conduct research on ocean life. Marées, who followed developments there with great interest and who knew Dohrn from his Jena days, met with him in Dresden in 1873 to discuss the decoration of the institute's library and the main hall which was the focus of its social life. This was a very important commission for Marées, whose financial and artistic security had just been shaken by the dissolution of his long and close relationship with Count Schack, his Munich patron. Unfortunately the building of the institute exhausted its funds, leaving nothing for the artist's fee or even for the cost of materials. Marées, obsessed by his new project, went to Konrad Fiedler, a prosperous friend and critic who greatly admired his art. Fiedler reluctantly agreed to help, though he doubted whether his gifted but very slow working and perfectionistic friend was up to the decorative task that the large frescoes entailed. For Marées, the project meant a chance to see Italy again, the country to which his art owed so much.

Assisted by the sculptor, Adolf Hildebrand, who made many suggestions for the overall scheme and helped him integrate the frescoes into their architectural setting, Marées worked feverishly, completing a task that was to have taken two years in a matter of months. His grand frieze was an act of reverence to the humble people of Italy, its fishermen, peasants and fruitgrowers. Thirteen studies in oil had preceded work on the frescoes, and Marées was able to transfer their powerful brushwork with almost no loss of spontaneity to the fresco medium.

This painting, initially left behind in Naples with other sketches and studies, came into the possession of Hildebrand, who donated it to the Nationalgalerie in 1907.

DH

42

16 Hans von Marées (1837—1887)

The Golden Age (The Ages of Life), c. 1878.
Oil and tempera on panel, 98 × 87 cm.

The ages of life is a subject that goes back to Marées' work on the Naples frescoes in 1873. According to his biographer, Julius Meier-Graefe, the artist used to call this his "Orange Painting", in allusion to the orange harvesters he had portrayed in one of those frescoes and studies for it. His Italian experience led Marées to concentrate more and more on idyllic scenes in his paintings and drawings both – gentle groves peopled with figures, some nude, some clad, signifying an Arcadia free of work and care, figures whose proportions gradually began to take on that slenderness which Marées so admired in paintings of the Northern Italian Renaissance.

Though he was a notoriously slow and painstaking worker, as can be seen from the heavily layered paint in *The Golden Age*, Marées almost certainly finished this painting at a much later date than *The Rowers*. In any event, its unconventional and almost exclusive reliance on the human figure astonished his friends, and Arnold Böcklin was deeply and visibly moved by the painting, "as invariably happened with the finest works of art he had ever seen."

A number of preparatory drawings for *The Golden Age* exist (now at Wuppertal), in which Marées brought its composition and theme to a focus. Here, for the first time, he achieved that balance between realism and ideal in the figure which was to prove so influential for such later styles as Symbolism, Art Nouveau and early Expressionism. The almost classically structured composition is counterpointed by the sheer physical presence of the figures, which seem on the verge of breaking out of the picture plane.

Marées gave *The Golden Age* to Konrad Fiedler in 1878. It was then acquired by Mary Balling, Partenkirchen, and upon her death in 1919 entered the collection of the Nationalgalerie.   DH

17 Arnold Böcklin (1827—1901)

Self-portrait with Death as Fiddler, 1872.
Oil on canvas, 75 × 61 cm.

This is one of the most beautiful and striking self-portraits of any age, and is certainly Böcklin's most important. Interrupted by Death's tune, the artist stops working to listen . . . It is probably true, as many observers think, that Böcklin had initially portrayed himself alone, adding his "inspired vision" of Death later, under the impression of a picture attributed to Holbein which he must have seen at the Old Pinakothek in Munich, where he was living at the time. Taken from traditional Dance of Death iconography, the motif was also used by such later artists as Hans Thoma and Lovis Corinth. Thanks to the figure of Death, self-aggrandizement immediately becomes self-criticism – a *memento mori*, reminding the artist and us that though he may be at the peak of his fame, death looks over his shoulder, and that though his art may be eternal, life is not. Such symbolism surely was not without influence on artists like Edvard Munch, who once wrote that he valued Böcklin "more highly than all the artists of the present day."

Böcklin returned to the theme of death again and again throughout his career, as witnessed by such works as *Lamentation beneath the Cross* of 1876, the five versions of *Island of the Dead* he painted during the 1880s, and finally by his *War* of 1897.

Böcklin was elected to honorary membership in the Munich Academy of Arts in 1872, the date of his portrait. Nevertheless he continued to be attacked from all sides, and the wider his renown spread, the more vociferous his critics grew. This however did not prevent the Nationalgalerie from regularly acquiring Böcklin's work for its collection.

DH

18 Gustave Courbet (1819—1877)

The Wave (La Vague), 1870.
Oil on canvas, 112 × 144 cm.

One of the major French artists of the past century, Courbet decisively influenced not only a generation of his young countrymen – the early Claude Monet and Edouard Manet particularly – but many German artists such as Leibl and Thoma as well. Born in Ornans in 1819, he went in 1839 to Paris where he largely taught himself by copying old masters in the Louvre. In 1855 he exhibited forty paintings at his own pavilion outside the official art section at the Universal Exhibition; this show, self-assuredly and simply entitled *Realism*, made him the acknowledged leader of a new movement in art.

He painted a great range of subjects, from portraits to historic scenes, nudes to hunting events and landscapes, and a number of seascapes done on the coast of Normandy where he spent several summers. Though they were finished later in the studio, his many pictures of huge waves breaking on the beach go back to the summer of 1869 – the outbreak of war in 1870 prevented Courbet from taking his annual trip to the coast. Guy de Maupassant, writing on "The Life of a Landscape Painter" in *Gil Blas*, described the vehemence with which Courbet worked on these canvases, an excitement that communicates itself immediately to anyone who sees them. Cézanne, too, was fascinated by the incredible force and violence of these depictions of waves, an elemental threat that comes out particularly in the Nationalgalerie painting. This was Cézanne's reaction: "The great wave, the one in Berlin – wonderful, one of the discoveries of the century, much more alive, more arched, with a more poisonous green and a dirtier orange than the one in the Louvre, with its boiling foam emerging from the depths of time, its tattered sky and pale sharp brilliance. It's as though it were coming at you, you flinch – the whole room smells of spray."

AS

19 Wilhelm Leibl (1844—1900)

Dachau Woman with Child, 1873—74.
Oil on panel, 86 × 68 cm.

Leibl, whose art was long dismissed as picturesque and rustic, stood for a realism in nineteenth-century German painting which was closely allied to that of Courbet in France. The two artists knew and respected one another's work, and after they had met personally — 1869 in Munich — Courbet arranged an invitation to Paris for his young German colleague. *Dachau Woman with Child* was done at a period in Leibl's career when his encounter with French art had helped him to bring the painterly element in his work to a high degree of maturity.

Basically, two aspects of the painting determine its effect: its motif, a young peasant woman and child; and the sureness of touch with which the motif has been painted. In both, Leibl's first principle was honesty — honesty as regards the subject, which he believed must be depicted as frankly as possible, without artificial dramatization; and honesty in the use of the artist's means, brushes and paint.

A young woman, seated on a bench before a light-grey wall, has put her arm around her son's shoulder. They wear the traditional formal costume of the town of Dachau rather than everyday working clothes, and both look straight out at us, the mother with a certain critical reserve, her youngster quite candidly. Their self-awareness and composure is striking. Leibl underscored this purposely, in protest against the anecdotal coyness with which peasant life was still generally depicted at the time. Human beings and their real lives interested him, not artfully composed, supposedly typical bucolic scenes of the kind that made the reputation of such artists as Defregger. Leibl's woman and child are individuals, portrayed as they were; they stand for nothing beyond their own existence as human beings. This, a realism of the kind that Courbet fought for, is precisely what lends them a greater significance.

Leibl has handled the paint with a relaxed ease that gives the surface a satiny translucency. The brushwork evokes atmosphere and materials without being merely imitative. Leibl achieved this painterly style after a long period of working in heavy impasto applied in short, quick strokes, an approach derived from Courbet's work and probably also from Manet's, whose paintings he must certainly have seen in Paris.   LG

20 Claude Monet (1840—1926)

St. Germain l'Auxerrois, 1866.
Oil on canvas, 79 × 98 cm.

Writing to the management of the Louvre in 1865, Monet, then still a young, unknown artist, asked whether he could set up his easel in the colonnade room of the Perrault wing of the museum. Permission was granted, and over the next two years both he and Renoir painted views of Paris from that vantage point – the Gothic church of St. Germain l'Auxerrois to the east, the Quai du Louvre, and the Infantin Gardens, the last two of which were very similar views.

Monet's choice of motif may possibly have been suggested by photographs of the day; in the early 1860s Guervin had trained his camera on the church from exactly the same angle. Comparable views of the city do not turn up in the painting of the time, either in the work of Manet or in that of Jongkind, whose landscapes had a profound influence on Monet. The compact composition and elevated viewpoint of this scene are more reminiscent of the tourist views to be had from the top of church towers, or of eighteenth-century city panoramas

such as those of Canaletto. And like Canaletto, Monet has portrayed the life on this city square in general rather than in detail – the people promenading under the blossoming chestnut trees, only fleetingly suggested, remain anonymous, parts of a crowd.

The picture is dated 1866, but this date has been questioned on account of certain obvious inconsistencies in style. While the buildings and church with its rosette window and buttresses have been delineated with precision, down to the texture of the stone, the trees and milling figures are blurred and their contours dissolved, making them mere patches of colour in a play of shadows and lights. This heralds the principle of Impressionism – to see the outside world as a series of optical sensations first and of significances and things only second.

Monet probably antedated the canvas, since in a letter to his friend, the painter Frédéric Bazille, he wrote in 1867 that he and Renoir were still working on their views of Paris.   AS

21 Claude Monet (1840–1926)

Summer, 1874.
Oil on canvas, 57 × 80 cm.

In 1874 the Paris photographer, Nadar, put his studio on Boulevard des Capucines at the disposal of a group of young artists for their first joint exhibition. This group included Monet, Sisley, Renoir and Berthe Morisot, and since the jury of the annual Salons had rejected their work once too often they had decided to show it inofficially. The public was accordingly scandalized; the press immediately and sneeringly labelled their brand of painting Impressionism. A critic had gleaned this word from the title of one of the paintings on show, Monet's *Impression – Sunrise*.

Impressionism has since come to be widely considered one of the greatest periods in the history of art, and the painting illustrated here, done in that memorable year of 1874 and bearing all the traits of the style, is one of the most popular in our collection. Its subject is simple and unliterary – a fine day in summer outside Paris, on the broad, rolling meadows of the Ile de France. A light breeze ruffles the leaves and tall grass; the three women walking and resting there seem a part of nature. Monet has used the same loose, almost negligent brushwork to depict everything in the scene, whether grass, foliage or figures.

Rather than attempting to convey the feel of different substances and materials he has caught the way they appear to the eye in brilliant, shimmering sunlight. This dissolution of solid matter into its visual correlate is one of the key traits of Impressionism. Another is the overall lightness of tone in Impressionist works, which led to their being termed "paintings in light". Perhaps expressive of a joyful, optimistic view of life, this light even extends to the shadows, which rather than being given simply as dark zones are full of colour as well. The pale green shadows in the foreground here communicate a feeling of transience and continual change, an impression which is heightened by the evanescent brushwork and by the seemingly chance way in which the artist has chosen this particular section of a larger view.

AS

22 Pierre Auguste Renoir (1841–1919)

Summertime, 1868.
Oil on canvas, 85 × 59 cm.

Lise Tréhot and Renoir probably first met in 1865. She soon became his favourite model, and his mistress. He painted her portrait again and again – in a formal pose with a sunshade (now in the Folkwang Museum, Essen), holding a bouquet of flowers, sewing. Only a few years before they met, Renoir had finished his training as a decorator of porcelain and had decided to devote himself entirely to painting. He was still quite unknown, and the pictures he was able to exhibit at the Salon – not many, since the jury frequently rejected them – were just beginning to attract attention. Among his early supporters was the writer, Emile Zola, who had done a great deal to further Manet.

This picture of 1868, with its official title of *Summertime, or the Gypsy Girl,* went largely unnoticed when it was exhibited at the Salon. It shows Lise at the age of twenty, dressed as a gypsy, before a wall of deep green summer foliage painted in broad, free strokes. Her hair is down; the white blouse has slipped off her soft, round shoulder; her hands rest in her lap. It is an image of almost animal passivity, a calm sensuousness which speaks from every detail, down to the gentle expression and distracted glance.

In this regard, as well as in the classical, sculptural modelling of the volumes, Renoir's portrait is close to the paintings of women by Courbet and, in a wider sense, even to French painting of the eighteenth century. For unlike Monet, who was his very close friend at the time, Renoir felt a strong obligation to traditional painting and with it to classical figurative compositions. Throughout his lifetime his interest concentrated on representing the human figure and particularly, as here, the beauty of woman.

AS

23 Edouard Manet (1832–1883)

The Conservatory (Dans la serre), 1879.
Oil on canvas, 115 × 150 cm.

Unlike the other Impressionists, Manet placed great store in having his work shown at the annual Salons, and thus had to submit it – not always successfully – to the judgement of the jury. In 1879, two paintings were accepted, *Boating* of 1874 and *The Conservatory* of 1878–79. At the time Manet was living at Rosen's studio on rue d'Amsterdam. His two paintings were received fairly generously by the critics, who had blasted such earlier entries of his as *Olympia* and *Nana*. They praised his tasteful palette and what compared to earlier works was a true-to-life rendering of hands and heads, as well as his freshness of approach, which had nothing academic about it.

Concerning Manet's choice of subject – a couple in a conservatory – the critics had very little to say. It does seem innocent enough at first sight. An elegant lady and a man of the world – Madame and Monsieur Jules Guillemet, who ran a boutique on rue Saint-Honoré, modelled for them – are involved in a conversation much like one that Zola might have recorded in his novel, *La Curée*, or which might recall Monet's *The Bench* of 1873 or even Rubens' *Honeysuckle Bower*. But the real theme, as in other paintings of the 1870s, is the estrangement of the sexes.

This is emphasized by the way Manet has divided the composition both horizontally and vertically. The woman sits on the bench to the left, while he, an older man whose features resemble the artist's own, stands above and behind it to the right, leaning forward. On the backrest – a transparent but stable divider – their hands meet, but without touching, the tensest point of contact between them. The man has been characterized as the active pole, his fingers with cigar pointing towards his companion, his body inclined in her direction. His face is mobile, its expression seemingly about to change at any moment.

The woman remains unmoved. Her eyes turned apathetically away, she disregards his banter. Precious as the camelias whose pale rose tint matches her budlike lips, she says nothing, makes no gesture, conscious of her beauty and passively willing to be admired.

Thanks to a formal language almost archaic in its simplicity, Manet has here succeeded in transforming what might easily have been a trivial subject – a society couple talking in a conservatory – into a compelling evocation of patterns of human behaviour which remain valid far beyond his time.

AS

24 Edouard Manet (1832–1883)

A Bunch of Lilacs, c. 1882.
Oil on canvas, 54 × 42 cm.

During the last months of his life Manet painted a series of floral still-lifes, usually of roses or lilacs in a crystal vase, thus returning to a subject which he had already treated in 1864 and 1868. His earlier flower arrangements were much more opulent than the later ones, however, with strings of pearls and arabesques of lemon peel which revealed his admiration for both Courbet's brilliant painting and seventeenth-century Dutch still-lifes. In his late works, Manet moved up closer to his subject, making it more intimate and simple. The allegorical pearls recalling the beautiful transient vanities of this world had gone.

The austere black-white contrast and shallow pictorial space in *A Bunch of Lilacs* owe more to the Japanese prints which had been the fashion among Paris artists since mid-century (compare Manet's portrait of Zola, 1867–68, in the Jeu de Paume, Paris). But unlike the prints, vivid brushwork has brought these lilac blossoms to radiant life. They glow against the dark background, and the impression of reality is so strong that one can almost smell them.

This small canvas was once part of the collection of Carl and Félicie Bernstein, who in the 1880s became the first in Berlin to purchase works by Monet, Manet, Degas, Berthe Morisot and Sisley. It was at their home, where Berlin art and letters met – Adolph von Menzel, Theodor Mommsen, Ludwig Curtius, Max Klinger and Wilhelm von Bode were frequent guests – that Max Liebermann and Hugo von Tschudi first saw the latest French Impressionist paintings, convincing them to go to Paris where together they laid the groundwork for the fine collection in the Nationalgalerie. *A Bunch of Lilacs* was bequeathed by Mrs. Bernstein to the museum in 1909.   AS

25 Max Liebermann (1847–1935)

The Stevenstift in Leyden, 1889.
Oil on canvas, 78 × 100 cm.

The Stevenstift is a home where needy elderly citizens of Leyden can spend their old age, and in Liebermann's work, the motif belongs to that series of old men's homes and orphanages which from 1880 he depicted again and again. Apparently, what appealed to him about them was not only the long Dutch tradition of community welfare they stood for, but the organic unity of architecture, social life and nature they embodied.

Compared with earlier pictures on the same theme, this one, despite certain similarities in composition, reveals differences in emphasis. The figures, once large, centrally placed, and shown involved in the activities of communal life, have here been arranged along the far edge of the canvas, almost like accessories to the scene. The environment dominates, taking up over half the space; and the artist has lavished a great deal of care on its rendering, working up the masses of foliage with a palette knife and coarse brush.

This noticeable increase in the importance of the natural surroundings, together with his new impasto technique, point up a change in Liebermann's approach to the outside world. Those were the years in which the sharp, incisive drawing of his earlier work gave way to rapid, searching brushwork as he attempted to capture fleeting impressions in paint, years in which the bonds of human community became less central to his art than the phenomena of nature. Liebermann's belief in the just society whose works he had depicted for so many years had apparently been shaken, and he turned elsewhere for orientation. He found it in the French Impressionists, whose paintings he began avidly to collect. ME

26 Lovis Corinth (1858—1925)

Donna Gravida, 1909.
Oil on canvas, 95 × 79 cm.

Lovis Corinth was among the finest portrait painters of his time. With this portrait of his wife, Charlotte, done in 1909 shortly before the birth of their daughter, Wilhelmine, he achieved one of his psychologically most penetrating works.

Known facetiously among the members of the artist's family as *Charlotte Transfigured,* the portrait received its present title from Raphael's picture of the same name at Palazzo Pitti in Florence. As the sitter herself wrote, *Donna Gravida* was "in most people's judgement the happiest and most mature of the many portraits devoted to me."

Charlotte Berend was a student in Corinth's art school in Berlin who became his wife in 1903. Sympathetic to his aims and possessed of a deep understanding of his work, she was a devoted companion who helped Corinth particularly through the bouts of depression from which he frequently suffered. Corinth had moved to Berlin from Munich in 1900, where he quickly advanced into the first rank of those artists who were developing a special German brand of Impressionism. With Liebermann, Slevogt and others at the exhibitions of the Berlin Secession, he championed an Impressionist approach which for all its variety drew its fundamental strength from a painterly intuition for the sensuous qualities of colour.

The rich panorama of his portraits, most of them of family, friends and acquaintances, reveals Corinth's extraordinary capacity to empathize with others. His deep understanding of personality is complemented here by the intimate trust of the woman who shared his life.

As regards method, Corinth has applied the paint in broad, flowing strokes which seem to concentrate all their power in the face, treating figure and clothing in a sketchier, more general manner. Avoiding strong colour contrasts and accents, he has reduced his palette to a narrow range of delicate pastel hues. His wife's features, and especially her gaze, evoke something of the physical change she is going through, one of the most basic of all human experiences.   PK

27 Max Slevogt (1862–1932)

Still-life with Lemons, 1921.
Oil on canvas, 64 × 80 cm.

Slevogt, like Max Liebermann and Lovis Corinth, was among those artists who have come to be known as German Impressionists, and of the three, he was the youngest. They all had much less in common with French Impressionism than the label would suggest. Never primarily concerned with "painting in light," their point of departure was the late nineteenth-century realism of Wilhelm Leibl and his school. What they gained from Impressionism was above all its liberation of the brushstroke, the demand that the painting process itself must grow autonomous of the content transmitted. Corinth and Slevogt, unlike their French counterparts, employed this liberated stroke with Baroque verve and expressiveness.

Slevogt's *Still-life with Lemons* is a late work. With a virtuosity gained by decades of experience, it embodies principles that date from the last years of the nineteenth century in a period of the twentieth when the younger Expressionists had already outgrown their revolution and Cubism had advanced to international prominence.

In the art of both this and the previous century, still-life, on account precisely of its lack of narrative content, has allowed artists to give their painterly skills free rein. And this is just what Slevogt has done here. His arrangement of objects was not meant to convey any symbolic or allegorical meaning; what unites these things we see on a patterned brown tablecloth against a dark wall, is the fact that they are all used for making lemonade: a silver dish piled with lemons and a sugar bowl at the right, a glass decanter in the centre, and at the left a lemon press, a glass with spoon, and a squeezer with two lemon halves. Rather than having a composed look, the whole seems to have come together by accident and to have struck the artist as visually promising. He has rendered the shimmering highlights on the silver and glass, the snow-white sugar, the fresh lemons and embroidered cloth in vibrant brushwork which can be appreciated on its own, without reference to the things portrayed. Their form and substance have been transmuted into pure painting.

During the 1920s when he painted this picture, Slevogt thought of himself as a "visual animal," one of the few surviving representatives of that species of pure painters, with an eye that "sees full of imagination ... full of music, rhythm and intoxication."

LG

28 Edvard Munch (1863—1944)

Count Harry Kessler, 1906.
Oil on canvas, 200 × 84 cm.

After the turn of the century, portraits, and particularly full-length portraits, began to assume more and more importance in Munch's art. His work of the 1890s had already presaged the tendency apparent here to isolate the standing figure against a flat, indeterminate background.

Human life was Munch's great theme. His cycles of paintings and prints were symbolic homages to love and fulfilment, loneliness and death. His acute insight into the human psyche and its deepest impulses predestined Munch for portraiture, a field in which he achieved a frank and noble simplicity which paved the way for a coming generation of Expressionist artists. In this characterization of his friend, Count Harry Kessler, Munch has likewise held that so difficult balance between an almost monumental dignity and unforced, vital presence. Dispensing with every accessory and frill, he has concentrated solely on the personality of his model. What counted in this approach, which he brought to the highest degree of immediacy, were his power of characterization and a palette reduced to the simplest terms of only a few shades of colour.

Kessler faces us frontally, slender and imposing, a walking stick held nonchalantly behind his back. The colour contrast between the dark blue-violet of his suit, accented in red, and the yellows and ochres of the background could hardly be more striking. A variation of the yellow in the straw hat, a lemon-yellow shaded with green under the brim, creates a transition from dominating dark silhouette to background.

Count Kessler, whom Munch had met in Berlin back in the 1890s, was among the most tenacious and outspoken of his supporters in Germany. The self-confidence of a man of the world comes out very clearly in Munch's portrait. He has succeeded in conveying Kessler's elegant appearance without dandifying him, capturing both his sensitive intelligence and his pride of bearing. Those were the years during which Kessler, helped by Henry van de Velde, was resolutely confronting the people of Weimar with some of the best in modern art.   PK

29 Oskar Kokoschka (1886–1980)

The Vienna Architect Adolf Loos, 1909.
Oil on canvas, 74 × 91 cm.

In 1908–09, while still in his early twenties, Oskar Kokoschka painted a series of portraits whose well-nigh clairvoyant acuteness won him fame among a small circle of admirers in Vienna despite critical and public incomprehension. Among those portraits was this one of his friend, Adolf Loos. Loos, an architect and writer who with Peret, Wright and Behrens was one of the pioneers of modern architecture, found very little opportunity to build in Vienna aside from a few private houses whose clear cubic shapes were starkly effective. The year before he sat for this portrait, Loos had published his now-famous polemic, *Ornament and Crime*. He was the young Kokoschka's first important patron, got him portrait commissions, and in 1909 even paid his expenses for a trip to Switzerland.

The two had been close friends since 1908. As Kokoschka once wrote, "Loos was my Virgil, who led me through the heaven and hell of human experience ... I got to know him in 1908, and a year later, when I had already cut free of the Wiener Werkstätte, I painted him. I could hardly understand why Loos considered my paintings works of art, and put it down to flattery. He did strengthen me in my conviction not to pursue any routine or theory but try to find, in my painting, a basis for understanding my role in society – to achieve self-awareness."

The figure, seated with arms angled and hands clasped, has the shape of a rhombus fit into the long rectangular canvas, an unusual format in portrait painting. Emerging from the midnight blue background, figure and face with its planes tinged in reds and yellows seem to be in a state of nervous agitation; a tremor passes through the sinewy hands, evoked by powerful strokes that continue on without a break into the coat sleeves. Illumination from below lends the man a visionary aspect, picking out lines and causing the colours to pale. This light heightens even further the expressive force of Loos's tense, angular features.

PK

30 Emil Nolde (1867–1956)

Pentecost, 1909.
Oil on canvas, 87 × 107 cm.

In 1909, while living alone in the small village of Ruttebühl in Schleswig Holstein, Nolde suffered a severe case of poisoning that nearly killed him. On his recovery he did his first paintings on religious themes, one of the most famous of which is *Pentecost*.

Up to that year Nolde had painted landscapes, still-lifes of flowers, and portraits; the religious images inspired by his close call with death now became, and were to remain, a significant part of his work. Two of the first were *Last Supper* (now in the Copenhagen Museum) und *Pentecost*. In his memoirs, *Years of Struggle*, Nolde later recalled his experience: "I had followed an irresistible urge to depict profound spirituality, religion and meditation, but without consciously wanting to or realizing why . . . I painted and painted, hardly knowing whether it was day or night, or whether I was more man or artist. If I had been bound by the letter of the gospel or by petrified dogma, I do not believe I could have painted these deeply felt images, *Last Supper* and *Pentecost*, as convincingly as I did. I had to be artistically free – not have God before me like some ironbound Assyrian monarch but within me, hot and holy like the love of Christ. With *Last Supper* and *Pentecost* came the turn from superficial visual appeal to emotionally felt inner value. They were milestones."

Though written years later, this description still captures the ecstatic state which gave rise to Nolde's first religious paintings and which opened up to him one of the central themes of his lifework. The last sentence suggests the role which *Pentecost* played in the development of his style. Influenced by van Gogh and in close contact with the *Brücke* painters in Dresden, he used pure, brilliant colours, applying them to the canvas with unmitigated spontaneity. His religious works of 1910 brought a change in the direction of stability, and his increasingly planar images took on a monumentality that was almost archaic.

The fact that this picture was rejected for the 1910 show of the Berlin Secession – its president, Max Liebermann, had objected to it personally – led the young Expressionists to found their own, New Secession.

LG

31 Erich Heckel (1883—1970)

Landscape near Dresden, 1910.
Oil on canvas, 66.5 × 78.5 cm.

In 1905, three young Dresden students of architecture got together with some of their friends to form a group which they called *Die Brücke* – The Bridge. Their aim was nothing less than "to attract every element that is revolutionary and in ferment." Erich Heckel, Ernst Ludwig Kirchner and Karl Schmidt-Rottluff were the three students, and all of them had decided to give up their academic profession to become painters. They were the driving force in the group while it lasted; such others as Emil Nolde, Max Pechstein, Otto Müller and the Swiss artist, Cuno Amiet, belonged to it only for a time. What united these artists was a development that from naturalistic and symbolist beginnings around 1905, took them via Post-Impressionism and the influence of Gauguin and van Gogh to the French Fauves, culminating finally in their own planar style of clearly contoured, simple shapes in pure colours. 1910 was the year of fulfilment for *Die Brücke*; never again would each artist's personal touch contribute so harmoniously to a group style. This phase of their work is known as the Dresden style.

Heckel's *Landscape near Dresden* is a work of that culminating year. The scene is probably in Friedrichstadt, a suburb of the city where the *Brücke* artists had their studios at the time and several views of which Kirchner also painted. Heckel has treated the cityscape here in a direct and spontaneous manner that recalls a drawing more than a conventional, finished oil. The shapes have been filled out in broad, flowing strokes and contoured with graphic black lines. The new demands which artists have made on their medium ever since Impressionism, can be reduced for simplicity's sake to three. Each has something to do with liberating painting from the need to represent real appearances: first, the demand that the picture surface be considered autonomous, that is, as a flat plane whose flatness, rather than being denied by creating the illusion of three dimensions on it, should be accepted and valued as such. Second, the demand that paint be given its autonomy as well, as a substance that instead of being required to imitate other substances or materials should stand for itself alone and be used for its inherent expressive possibilities. And third, that the artist's temperament should be allowed free rein in the way he handles the brush and deploys his colours.

The 1910 paintings of *Die Brücke* brought a decisive breakthrough in all three areas.

LG

32 Karl Schmidt-Rottluff (1884−1976)

Farmyard at Dangast, 1910.
Oil on canvas, 86.5 × 94.5 cm.

With Heckel and Kirchner, Karl Schmidt-Rottluff was a founding member and leading talent of *Die Brücke* during its Dresden years. Like the suburban landscape by Heckel just described, his *Farmyard at Dangast* was executed in 1910.

Though they were united by the stylistic development which they all went through, each of the *Brücke* artists retained his personal approach, as a comparison of their paintings shows. While Heckel and Kirchner produced images dominated by violent agitation or vibrating with nervous sensibility, Schmidt-Rottluff achieved a special balance and calm of which this canvas is a characteristic example. Using the same painterly means with which Heckel had evoked movement and tension, he has created the impression of a tranquil equilibrium.

All the elements of his motif – the buildings and trees of a farmyard, part of a larger whole – have been composed such that no one of them overpowers the next. The softly contoured colour fields flow into one another, forming an ornamental pattern of harmonious clarity.

Schmidt-Rottluff has emphasized the flat plane of the canvas even more by employing colours of equal brilliance in both background and foreground, which has the effect of bringing the far buildings and trees forward and tying them into the overall pattern. Used pure and unmixed, these colours designate objects only in a very general sense. The sky may be blue, the trees green and the roofs red, but the sunny spots on the ground are red as well and the shadows an intense blue – neither, certainly, as it would look in reality.

Besides the city and its environs as represented here by works of Kirchner and Heckel, rural scenes were an important subject for all the *Brücke* artists, who used regularly to spend part of the year in the country. Between 1907 and 1912, Schmidt-Rottluff and Heckel often went to Dangast together, a village on the North Sea coast near Oldenburg, and before that K. Schmidt-Rottluff had worked with Emil Nolde on Alsen, a Danish island in the Baltic. The North and Baltic Sea coasts were to remain Schmidt-Rottluff's favourite landscapes.

LG

33 Ernst Ludwig Kirchner (1880–1938)

Belle Alliance Square, Berlin, 1914.
Oil on canvas, 96 × 85 cm.

The two foregoing paintings by Erich Heckel and Karl Schmidt-Rottluff are examples of that *Brücke* style of 1910, the phase during which the stylistic similarity among the artists in the group was highest. The next years saw them diverge, each following his own personal bent. After they moved from Dresden to Berlin in 1911 – the German capital certainly had a freer and more cosmopolitan air than the Saxon residence town – the group began to disperse, and by 1913 it was a thing of the past.

Kirchner is now considered the finest painter of the *Brücke*, and he is perhaps best known for the scenes of big-city life which he depicted so well – the streets packed by day with throngs of office-workers and the hectic attractions of night, the vaudeville shows and circus, nightclubs and brothels. With an almost visionary hypersensibility he traced the restless pulse of the city and transmuted it into imagery.

His painting of *Belle Alliance Square* shows Kirchner at a time when the Dresden style had already made way for his very personal Berlin style. Characteristic of this new approach is the way in which he has depicted the square from above, tipping it forward to open out the surrounding buildings like a fan. His drawing has become sharp and brittle; his palette has lost its former brilliance and harsh contrasts of complementary colours in favour of more subdued tones. This limited range of colour values is quite typical of Kirchner's paintings of Berlin, as is the nervous crosshatching of the brushwork, evocative of the hectic pace of urban life. The image is dominated by the square hemmed in with facades, dwarfing the figures – tiny faceless people who move with a strange, angular awkwardness.

Belle Alliance Platz was once a major intersection at the south end of Friedrichstrasse. When Berlin was divided it lost its function and has since been completely rebuilt. Known today as Mehringplatz, all that remains of the prewar square is the Column of Victory in its centre, which in reality is much more modest than monumental.   LG

35 George Grosz (1893—1959)

Pillars of Society, 1926.
Oil on canvas, 200 × 108 cm.

Grosz was a bar owner's son who after his studies and military service joined Berlin Dada early on. He made a name for himself with print portfolios and books that were harshly critical of German society during the first years of the Weimar Republic (*Face of the Ruling Class*, 1921; *Philistines' Mirror*, 1925). His *Pillars of Society* is a resumé of the character types he had developed in innumerable lithographs and drawings. Encouraged by Heinrich Vogeler, a German painter living in Moscow who told Grosz that artists there were working out a new "synthetic realism", he painted what has since come to be known as an Allegory of the German Nation.

The figure in the foreground personifies chauvinism. Encased in a business suit, he brandishes beer glass and duelling sword and displays his old fraternity colours on his tie. Judging by the monocle and the decoration in his lapel he is a former cavalry officer; a ghostly rider surrounded by paragraph symbols characterize him as a desk jockey and pedant who would not think of budging from the letter of the law.

To his left is an embodiment of journalism, middle-class and always flexibly middle-of-the-road but full of latent aggression. He grips his pencil like a dagger, the newspapers are flecked with blood, and even the palm frond he holds as a sign of conciliation is blood-stained. The quality of the man's thinking – his features recall Hugenberg, the Weimar newspaper boss's – is summed up by his chamber-pot helmet.

On the right, finally, a symbolic parliamentarian rests his elbow on the portal of the Reichstag. Possibly inspired by Hindenburg, the figure holds a flag with the colours of the former Reich, and the placard on his chest reads "Socialism is Work," a Social Democratic campaign slogan of the period directed against the Communist Party's strike appeals. Grosz has described the state of political thought at the time as literally excremental.

The black-robed figure hovering over these three is certainly a personification of the Church. Preaching forgiveness and peace, he simultaneously gives his blessing to their actions and to the company of Reichswehr soldiers burning and pillaging at the upper right. Here Grosz alludes to the defeat of the revolution and the civil war that raged during Weimar's first difficult years.

Grosz's social criticism certainly reached its culmination in this painting. The following years saw him gradually turning away from subjects of this kind, and after his emigration to the United States, he was never to return to them.   ME

36 Otto Dix (1891–1961)

The Art Dealer Alfred Flechtheim, 1926.
Mixed media on panel, 120 × 80 cm.

Alfred Flechtheim, with a gallery in Düsseldorf since 1919 and a second in Berlin since 1922, was one of the best-known German art dealers of the period. His gallery on Lützowplatz in Berlin was devoted particularly to exhibiting and selling those modern French paintings which were Flechtheim's main interest. Berlin audiences got to know the work of Matisse, Braque, Léger, Gris, Picasso and Derain primarily through him.

Dix had come to Berlin in late 1925, on the initiative of his dealer, Nierendorf. Who commissioned his portrait of Flechtheim is still not certain. He has characterized this strategist of the international art market entrenched among some of his treasures. On the wall behind him hangs a still-life by Juan Gris, which Dix has embellished with his own initial and date. His left hand resting on the frame of a Braque, Flechtheim has spread the fingers of his right across a Picasso drawing such that only a few lines of it are visible. By this gesture Dix suggests that Flechtheim speculated with erotic drawings in order to awaken the interest of potential buyers in more substantial works.

Though Dix's portrayal amounts almost to a wanted poster and he thought Flechtheim "avaricious and decadent," he certainly also was hitting out here at the ignorance of a buying public who were interested in other than aesthetic experiences when they walked into a gallery. Seen in this light, Dix's portrait shows Flechtheim to be not only a clever businessman who was all too aware of his clientele's weak spots but a man who did not always find it easy to overcome public resistance to the Cubist painting he admired and fought for. Dix himself was not enamoured of Cubism, as his ironic signature indicates – I could do a Gris as good as this one any day, it seems to say.

ME

37 Laszlo Moholy-Nagy (1895–1946)

Composition Z VIII, 1924.
Distemper on canvas, 114 × 132 cm.

With Moholy-Nagy, the Hungarian artist whom Walter Gropius brought to the Bauhaus in 1923, a new brand of creative thinking entered this key Weimar art school – socially committed, scientifically oriented, experimental, and devoted to new materials and methods that revolutionized traditional painting. His experience of the First World War, as he wrote in 1919, had "awakened my responsibility to society," prompting him to ask, "Is it right to become an artist in an age of social transformation?" His answer was yes, since he realized that his talent was for expressing "vital and creative forces through light, colour and form."

He had studied with Sandór Bortnyik at the Mühely in Budapest, a school that was oriented along similar lines to the Bauhaus, then joined a group led by Lajos Kassák, who had made the journal *MA* into a major forum of discussion for Constructivist art. "The new mass age," wrote Moholy-Nagy in 1922, "needs Constructivism because it needs a foundation that does not rest on illusions." He was able to put this principle into practice at the Bauhaus, and later, at the New Bauhaus in Chicago, to give it additional scientific underpinning. His experimental methods included kinetics, light, film, photography, the stage – he had worked with Piscator in Berlin prior to 1933 – and industrial design. Like Marcel Breuer and Herbert Bayer, he was interested in every area of design for modern living.

The painting in our collection, done at the Bauhaus, is a good example of Moholy-Nagy's attempts to lend a flat surface a third, spatial dimension without the aid of conventional perspective. The unprimed canvas contributes to its look of an object rather than a picture, a characteristic trait of much of the art of that period.

DH

38 Paul Klee (1879–1940)

The Ships' Departure, 1927.
Oil on canvas, 51 × 65.5 cm.

Klee taught at both the Weimar Bauhaus, from 1921 to 1930, and at Dessau after the school's move there. His daily instruction in both preliminary and master courses led him to reflect on his own creative methods, to record them systematically, and finally to publish a number of his essays and lecture notes under the title *Visual Thinking* (*Das bildnerische Denken*). In the chapter entitled "A Creative Confession," which goes back to the year 1918, Klee wrote: "A man of ancient times as sailor in a ship, enjoying the voyage and appreciative of the vessel's ingenious comforts. The ancients depicted such things accordingly. And now, what a modern fellow experiences when he walks along a liner's deck: 1. His own motion; 2. the motion of the ship, which may be in the opposite direction; 3. direction and speed of the current; 4. the earth's rotation; 5. its orbit; 6. the orbits of moon and planets around it. The result – a system of motions in the universe with the Ego on the liner in its centre."

Here, the primary motion, that of the ship, is indicated by a forceful red arrow. Progress through space and time – Klee's system of motions in the universe – has been symbolized by the overlapping sails, with each sail marking a finite point in the ships' course, just as the blue semicircles at the lower right signify the path of the waves.

Klee has ordered and simplified these natural and man-made phenomena, giving them abstract shapes that transcend the individual and accidental. His employment of colour has a similar purpose – bright blue has been used for the cold, lifeless water and the distant, burnt-out sun; warm yellows, pinks and reds, by contrast, appear only in the ships, those man-created means of transportation whose forward motion is the first premise of civilization.

AS

39 Giorgio de Chirico (1888–1979)

The Great Metaphysician, c. 1923–24.
Oil on canvas, 110 × 80 cm.

Giorgio de Chirico was an Italian born in Greece, where his father worked as a railway surveyor. While studying in Munich he discovered Schopenhauer and Nietzsche, and the art of Böcklin and Klinger, who markedly influenced his early style. The great change in his life came with service in a field hospital in Ferrara; for him as for many others, World War I brought European civilization to an end.

This experience is strikingly embodied in *The Great Metaphysician* of 1916 (Museum of Modern Art, New York). The painting in our collection is a later and purposely antedated version of the same motif in which de Chirico, the proto-Surrealist, brought his metaphysical painting to a point. By the term metaphysical, de Chirico meant that which lies behind and between things and remains invisible to the objective eye – their essence, in a word. By spiriting things out of their normal context and into strange new ones, or by reversing or confusing their familiar dimensions, he attempted to lay open the enigmatic core of real appearances.

One of these means of estrangement was the exaggerated perspective with which he has depicted this open plaza. A monument rises in its centre, composed of objects and implements that once served some useful purpose, such as measuring, dividing or decorating, activities that had once contributed to the meaningful and beautiful order of the man-made world. Now these instruments have conglomerated into a confusing and mysterious collection which has almost engulfed their creator and master, the Metaphysician. He has become a prisoner of his own creations, a slave to his tools, a lifeless mannequin.

In his novel, *Hebdomeros*, de Chirico wrote in 1929: "In face of the increasingly materialistic and pragmatic orientation of our age ... it is not obtuse to imagine a future social order in which those who live only for intellectual pleasures will no longer have a right to their place in the sun. The writer, the thinker, the dreamer or poet, the metaphysician or observer of life ... whoever asks riddles, evaluates ... will have become an anachronistic figure, doomed, like the ichthyosaurus and the mammoth, to disappear from the surface of the earth."

ME

40 René Magritte (1898—1967)

L'idée fixe, 1927.
Oil on canvas, 81 × 115 cm.

While in his early work he illustrated the incongruity of reality and fiction usually by combining diverse and conflicting points of view in a single image, about 1927 or '28 Magritte began to concentrate for the first time on confronting the names of things with their images. For him, name and image represented two, often completely unrelated ways of designating an object, abstractions neither of which were equivalent to it. Perhaps the most famous example of this concern is his painting, *Use of Language*, where an image of a pipe is captioned, "This is not a pipe." A painted pipe cannot be picked up, stuffed with tobacco and smoked; its image may appear real, but it can never actually be real.

The painting in our collection adds another dimension to the puzzle. It consists of four symmetrically arranged images, painted in a traditional manner, each of which represents an excerpt from the real world – a scene in the depths of a forest, a section of sky, a section of a facade, and a hunter apparently waiting for game in an unlikely setting. Though each is painted quite conventionally and realistically, their combination is highly unconventional; four isolated slices of reality that do not add up to a comprehensible image of reality. Combined more logically, they might result in a landscape with building and the figure of a hunter, but divided as they are with heavy black lines, they remain mutually isolated and, as a whole, without clear meaning. This is confusing, and it gives rise to a feeling of anxiety.

Each separate section is disquieting, too; danger seems to lurk in the silent wood, behind the curtains, even in the sky. The constricted view we are given of each of these things only adds to the anxiety, a feeling perhaps embodied in the hunter who, isolated as well, appears to be waiting in the deepening twilight for something to hold on to, on which to concentrate, a target to shoot at, which would at least relieve the tension and put his familiar world back in joint.

But that is exactly what cannot happen in this picture because he himself is part of a fragmented composition which negates the continuum of reality, giving rise to confusion and fear. To be free, he would have to escape from this system whose form and symmetry suggest some concealed connection. Yet recalling other Magritte paintings in which a hunter likewise appears, one begins to wonder whether he was ever intended to escape.

ME

41 Max Ernst (1891−1976)

The Chosen Bride of Evil, 1928.
Oil on canvas, 198 × 303 cm.

Two constants may be traced through Max Ernst's so disquieting universe of contradictions: first, a never-ending metamorphosis of human, animal and vegetable forms, and secondly, that birdlike creature which turns up again and again with its strange blend of exuberant fun and demonic threat. Both constants converge in the legendary beast which the artist has ironically dubbed *The Chosen Bride of Evil* (L'élue du Mal).

This is one of the most memorable images in the series of *Bird Monuments* which Max Ernst began a few years before. Evil's fiancée is an awesome parody, a creature as much amphibian as she is bird, equipped with an alligator's long curving teeth and with majestic pinions reminiscent of the legendary Giant Roc. Nor do the uncertainties end here – the beast's green colour, the long leaflike projection on its head, and the sharp red tongue recall certain members of the cactus family. And as far as the human realm is concerned, the two-headed charmer even wears breastplates that cast an illusionary shadow.

Its hybrid shape was possibly inspired by an illustration in some book of natural history showing extinct flying lizards of the Mesozoic Age, batlike creatures with huge jaws lined with conical teeth. The monster's tiny eyes seem disembodied, floating like planets or stars in space, whose depths are accentuated by the cankerous red moon below. The impression of unearthliness is heightened still further by the desert waste at the bottom of the scene.

This landscape is like a premonition of the desert in Arizona where Max Ernst was to settle almost two decades later. One recalls André Breton's remark that the artist's paintings often contained things that did not yet exist and foreshadowed events to come.

Birds played an enigmatic role in Max Ernst's life from a very early age. He himself once traced this fascination back to the day when his sister Loni was born. At the very moment of her birth, his beloved pet, a pink cockatoo, died, a coincidence which he was never able to forget and which awakened his lifelong interest in occult phenomena.

PK

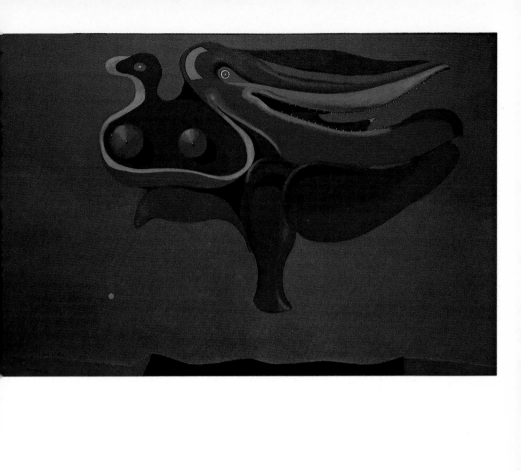

42 Fernand Léger (1881–1955)

The Two Sisters, 1935.
Oil on canvas, 162 × 114 cm.

Until recently, the Nationalgalerie possessed only one small, early canvas by Léger – *Composition* of 1920 – which was not really representative of the achievement of one of the finest of twentieth-century artists.

After beginnings influenced by Picasso, Léger worked out his own, very personal version of Cubism which on account of the pipelike forms he employed has been called Tubism. Like the Constructivist artists his aim in creating this style was to overcome the two-dimensionality of the picture plane by depicting objects concretely, surrounded by space. He carried his interest beyond the studio by designing colour schemes for city streets and squares, and in the late 1920s and early 1930s the scaffoldings and constructions of his paintings began to be populated with human figures, building workers and engineers and muscular women, images that for all their artificiality reflected a new faith in the simple labours of human hands.

In contrast to such other streams of the period as Neue Sachlichkeit in Germany with its austerity and recourse to nineteenth-century precision and themes, and to the socially critical realism of Grosz and Dix, Léger treated his subject-matter with an almost classical simplicity and balance. In this he resembled both Picasso and Matisse, but without the storytelling verve of the one or the decorative bent of the other. Foremost in his mind was always the desire to express, if not to recreate, the idea of human dignity.

The Two Sisters is an excellent example of this concern which was so characteristic of Léger's mature work. It is a major painting, acquired from the collection of Steven Hahn, the New York art dealer. Its purchase has enabled the Nationalgalerie to document, at the highest level of quality, the tradition of French painting from Courbet to Manet, Monet and Renoir down into the twentieth century.

DH

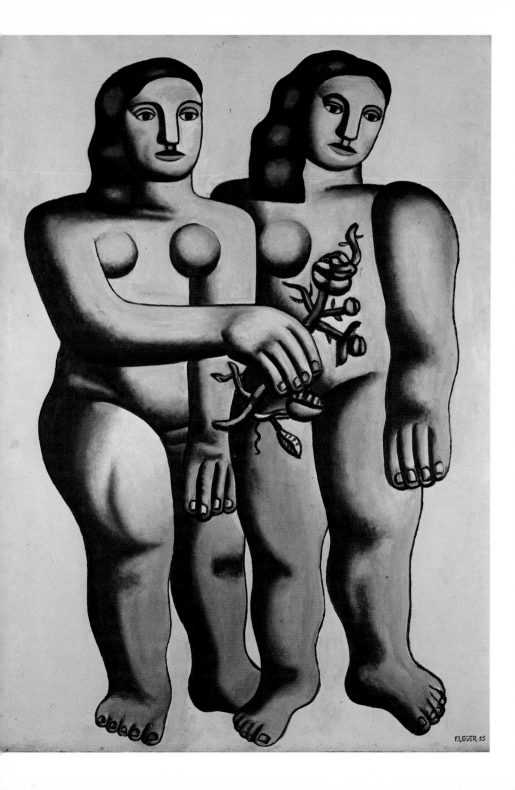

43 Max Beckmann (1884—1950)

Death, 1938.
Oil on canvas, 121 × 176.5 cm.

Beckmann ranks among the most significant German artists of the interregnum. After Post-Impressionist beginnings in 1904—05, he turned to Expressionism about 1909 and then, deeply affected by the horrors of World War I, he began to paint in that inimitable style that was to mark his work from then on. He filled his canvases to the bursting point with figures and fragments of experience, creating a new reality out of chaos.

The paintings *Birth* and *Death* are companion-pieces executed in 1937 and 1938 in Amsterdam where Beckmann, branded a degenerate artist by the Nazis, lived in exile. It has been said that the artist began this canvas when he heard of the death of Kirchner, though he did not know him personally. It represents the visions of a dying woman who sees the events of her past life recapitulated, but in a strangely jumbled form. To depict the undepictable Beckmann has made use of images from Anglo-Indian theosophy, configurations that are too complex in associations to be explained here in detail. In what follows we shall rely on Friedhelm Fischer, who has provided invaluable pointers to their interpretation. The dead woman lies on a kind of bier in the centre with a nurse and assistant at her feet and an odd, six-footed figure of Indian aspect standing beside her. Seemingly floating out of the scene at the right is an incongruous couple, a woman embraced by a fish. The figures at the top are upside down, defying the law of gravity – at least as it holds on earth – and next to a male choir with monstrous triple faces a variety of strange hybrid creatures prance across the boards of a stage.

A rough idea of what this enigmatic image means can be had from the notion of Kama-Loka, the first stage after death. Dying is an arduous process in which the soul passes through many phases, and Kama-Loka, pictured here, involves two experiences – first, remembrances of one's past life, and secondly, a cleansing of the soul of all elements of impurity and disorder. Kama-Loka moreover designates the realm of desire, where the laws of space and time break down, and where the desires and passions that remain beyond death – symbolized here especially by the woman-fish couple – lead to a reincarnation. The fact that Beckmann has chosen a woman to represent death and reincarnation seems doubly significant, the female principle being the life-giving principle and women, to a greater degree than men, having always figured as objects of lust and desire.

AS

44 Giorgio Morandi (1890–1964)

Still-life with Bottles, 1940.
Oil on canvas, 47 × 52.8 cm.

Morandi was a solitary figure in twentieth-century art. For decades he painted nothing but still-lifes, arrangement after arrangement of the same things on a table top. Yet his career had begun with involvement in most every international art movement of the day, from post-Cézanne landscapes to Cubism and Futurism and finally Italian metaphysical painting. It was this last style that provided the solid foundation for his still-lifes to come, for it defined that certain approach to the inanimate things which Morandi untiringly depicted.

In contrast to most still-lifes from the inception of this genre in the late sixteenth century, Morandi's compositions are based on unprepossessing things raised to a degree of artificiality that divests them of real associations and anecdotal elements of every kind. Though his objects are certainly individual, that is, they possess a definite, unmistakably objective character and appear in arrangements each of which differs from the next, this individuality is itself artificial, limited to the medium in which they have been represented and without reference beyond it. They are sufficient unto themselves.

In order to achieve this absolute neutrality as regards their origin and function, Morandi painted the bottles and jugs and vessels that he collected in his studio with thick, dull colours, thus giving them that same inanimate, artless look in reality as they have in his paintings.

Thanks to this artificial isolation Morandi was able to concentrate on a purely pictorial problem – the interrelationship of his objects in space and its depiction on a plane surface. What lay behind his approach, as Werner Haftmann has written, was ". . . a profound experience of the enchanted stillness of form and the poetry of simple objects."　　LG

45 Karl (Carl) Hofer (1878–1955)

The Black Rooms, 1943.
Oil on canvas, 149 × 110 cm.

In the empty, cell-like rooms of the painting's title, four men move like phantoms to the beat of a drum. The atmosphere is oppressive; apparently there is no way out of this enclosure, nor do the men seem to have any goal. They are like prisoners in a penetentiary, their cells barred but interpenetrating and all the more disquieting for having windows of different heights and incomplete walls. The men trapped in this maze have become anonymous creatures, cut off completely from the outside world.

A tall figure rises before one of the windows, blocking out the view, in an attitude which like that of the others has something compulsive about it. He takes as little notice of the others as they do of him, as if they were all caught in a trance. The drummer alone seems awake, on the point of announcing some dire event, driving the others to hectic aimless activity.

Hofer painted the first version of this nightmarish vision as early as 1928. This and two further foreboding works, *Yellow Dog Blues* and *Self-portrait with Demons*, done at about the same period, tore a sudden gap in the detached world of classical subjects which Hofer had painted up to then. He had had a clear view of the "poisoned political horizon", as he called it, and in *The Black Rooms* he created a compelling metaphor for what the future was soon to bring. Commenting on this element of premonition that so often found its way into his imagery, Hofer wrote: "The artist is a spiritual seismograph who predicts imminent disaster. This has happened not only in my own works."

When his studio burned out in 1943, destroying the first version of the painting, Hofer immediately began work on this repetition, based on a photograph. "Nostradamus' millenia-old prophecy about the birds with wings of bronze ravaging the earth with fire, has begun to come true," the artist recorded. "In March 1943, during the first major air raid on Berlin, my studio went up in flames with all my paintings and everything that connected me with my past life. Four days later I was standing at a new easel with new materials in a little room of my apartment – which likewise fell prey to fire in November of that same year." PK

46 Salvador Dali (b. 1904)

Mrs. Isabel Styler-Tas (Melancolia), 1945.
Oil on canvas, 65.5 × 86 cm.

During the 1940s, which Dali spent in the United States, he accepted a number of commissions to paint portraits of well-known society people, among them Helena Rubinstein. His portrait of Isabel Styler-Tas, daughter of the Amsterdam jeweller, Louis Tas, was done in 1945, when she was living in Beverly Hills.
Dali has characterized his model as rather forbiddingly unapproachable, an impression heightened by the Surrealist expanse behind her. The composition is quite evidently based on Piero della Francesca's *Duke and Duchess of Urbino*, though Dali has replaced the abundant domains in the background of that picture with a plain that looks more like a dream-vision of purgatory. And unlike Piero's twin portrait of man and wife, Mrs. Styler has been made to confront a petrified image of herself, a precipice difficult of ascent.
The large brooch on her dress bears the head of Medusa, the legendary Gorgon whose aspect turned anyone who saw it into stone. All of these allusions, like the subtitle which Dali gave to the painting, Melancolia, recalling the famous engraving by Dürer in which he interpreted melancholy as a temperament and a state of mind, must be seen as ironic commentary on one of the wealthiest society women of the day.

AS

47 Wols (Alfred Otto Wolfgang Schulze) (1913–1951)

Painting, 1946–47.
Oil on canvas, 80 × 80 cm.

Wolfgang Schulze worked as a musician and photographer before the experience of confinement in a French internment camp brought him to painting. He always referred to himself as a self-taught amateur rather than a professional artist, but he was nevertheless influenced by modern art, particularly by French Surrealism.

Surrealist writers and artists, combatting the rationalist orientation of traditional art, emphasized the significance of the subconscious mind in the creative process and made it a central theme of their work. One of the Surrealists' most revolutionary methods was what they termed "automatism". By drawing and painting with extreme rapidity they hoped to reduce the influence of conscious thought and thus of rational control on the flow of imagery, letting it be dictated only by the promptings of the unconscious. The artist was to become a medium for those experiences of the outside world which had collected and condensed within the dark regions of his mind. To attain to this "inner view" and record it in the act of painting was the aim which Wols pursued as well.

His compositions came about more or less by chance, but it was a chance subject to unconscious control. In this approach, accidents that happen in the course of painting are positive events, enabling the artist to depict what Werner Haftmann once called "that intermediate realm where the real and the imaginary cease to appear mutually exclusive." In this sense Wols bridged the gap between painting content and the act of its creation, bringing them into an existential unity which every spectator can re-experience for himself.

MP

106

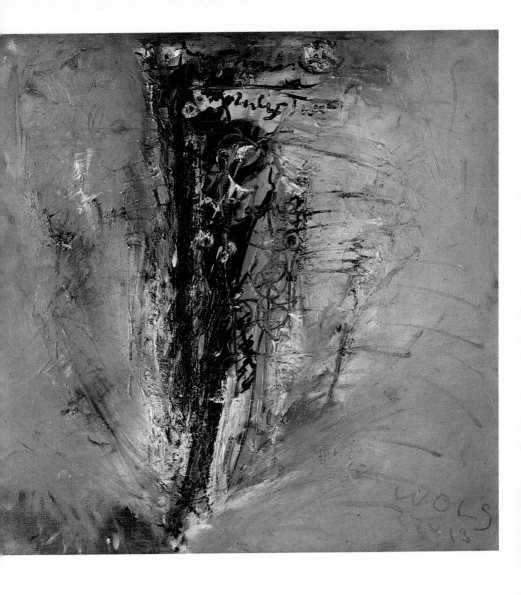

48 Ernst Wilhelm Nay (1902—1968)

Mélisande, 1948.
Oil on canvas, 90 × 60 cm.

The name Mélisande takes us into the realm of legend and myth, that bucolic domain where most of Nay's compositions of 1948 had their home, as evidenced by such other of their titles as *Cythera, Oberon, Prometheus* and *David*. Mélisande is a symbolic figure, a beautiful demigoddess whose origin is obscure but whose presence brings no good. She appears in a play by Maeterlinck, a fairy-tale that probably goes back to an old Flemish or Breton legend; set to music by Debussy, it was performed in 1902 under the title *Pelléas et Mélisande*.

Whether Nay was alluding here to the legend or to Debussy's opera must remain open. He spent most of the war years in France, where both legend and opera were current. In any event, the painting cannot be understood in an illustrative sense. Nay was concerned here to find an equivalent for the mythological figure in form and colour. The demonic fireworks of his combination of green, red, yellow and pink might suggest the supernatural, magical element in the tale, while the dark brown and black rectangular and triangular shapes evoke the forest depths where Mélisande was found.

The longer one looks, the more certain identifiable motifs crystallize out of the image – a house gable with a window like the one out of which Mélisande gazed with her long golden hair, a face, and more. The painting belongs to a phase of transition in the artist's work. Over the following years his interest turned gradually away from semi-abstraction with objective referents and towards colour, which he liberated more and more from the tectonic structures into which it was initially bound.   AS

49 Willi Baumeister (1889–1955)

Montaru 8, 1953.
Oil on hardboard, 130 × 100 cm.

Like Oskar Schlemmer, Baumeister studied with Adolf Hoelzel and Otto Meyer-Amden. During the 1920s he worked in a semi-abstract figurative style which he hoped to apply to wall-filling murals, but the times were not propitious – he too was soon branded a degenerate artist by the Nazis.

In the seclusion of his studio Baumeister gradually expunged every figurative and objective reference from his imagery. By the end of the 1930s he had arrived at his "ideograms", spiritual symbols which bore a certain resemblance to prehistoric, Assyrian or Sumerian hieroglyphs and in a few cases also to Chinese wordsigns. The following years saw him improvising in more or less abstract terms on mythical themes such as Gilgamesh, or, like Miró, on the workings of the subconscious mind made visible in the act of painting.

This is the context in which his *Montaru* series of 1953–54 belongs. Though the word Montaru may evoke primordial associations, it was Baumeister's own, derived from the French word *mons,* for mountain, and signifying to the artist the Mount Ararat of the Bible. These images, some of them upright and some horizontal in format, are dominated by expansive, irregularly shaped black fields with ragged edges which float on the painting surface like continents surrounded by bright-coloured elongated shapes.

"The root fibres and other outgrowths," wrote Baumeister, "indicate motion through time. Thanks to them and to the coloured protuberances emerging from behind the black, this dark body is prevented from being seen as a void, as a dimension of depth. The black has to be matt" – this he achieved by rubbing the paint with buttermilk – "because the slightest reflection on it would be enough to ruin the desired effect."

Baumeister wrote in another place about the formal and philosophic aspects of this series: "The *Montaru* paintings are a good example of the appearance of large forms as central forms. You might call them monumental solo forms in the image centre, except that this is counteracted by one thing – besides its monumental and soloistic character this black centre also possesses the quality of nothingness, vacuum, emptiness . . . Thus action and reaction are induced by a single form."

AS

50 Serge Poliakoff (1906–1969)

Composition with Red and Yellow Shapes, 1963.
Oil on canvas, 157 × 127 cm.

Serge Poliakoff was born in Moscow in 1906. His family was highly cultured and acquainted him at an early age with the artistic and intellectual life of the period. Music was his first interest, leading him to study classical guitar, in which he became so proficient that he was able to accompany his aunt, a famous singer, on many concert tours throughout Europe. In 1919 Poliakoff emigrated to Paris, where he taught himself to paint. During a stay in London he attended the Slade School of Art for a short time, but the main influences on his work came after his return to Paris – the art of Kandinsky and especially that of Robert and Sonia Delaunay, whose weekly painting classes he attended regularly. Though like most of his contemporaries he was looking for a pathway to abstraction, his art diverged from theirs early on. "I believe in abstract art," he wrote, "because it allows one to develop in freedom of spirit."

While Delaunay in particular worked out his new vocabulary of forms by abstracting from real objects and attempted to employ this vocabulary within the traditionally composed image, Poliakoff built his pictures up of non-objective colour fields which had no referent in the visible world. These fields were neutral in terms of content, and in combination produced a harmonious, self-contained pictorial structure.

He reduced his compositions to a few basic elements, schemes focussed in the centre of the image, as in the present painting. Irregular fields of translucent, seemingly vibrating colour have been juxtaposed and interlocked in no apparent order; they seem to move from the edges of the canvas towards the centre, an impression heightened by the growing intensity of colour from the periphery inwards. This rhythmic structure recalls that of some natural organism, developing logically and nowhere interrupted by disturbances or irregularity.

Seen individually, on the other hand, each shape appears to advance or recede in space with respect to its neighbour, though they all fall back into the overall surface pattern as soon as we focus on the whole. Thanks to this absolute harmony of colour fields and composition, the parts and the whole, Poliakoff's paintings emanate tranquillity and profound spiritual calm. As the artist himself once said of abstract art, it ". . . comes more from the spirit and goes more deeply into the spirit."

MP

51 Mark Rothko (1903—1970)

Reds Number 5, 1961.
Oil on canvas, 177.8 × 160 cm.

Rothko, born in 1903, went to the United States with his family in 1913. He became with Barnett Newman and Morris Louis one of the most compelling representatives of a post—1945 approach to art which raised colour to an absolute quality. Like many American artists Rothko was influenced early in his career by Surrealist painting, a key movement in the United States thanks to the many European artists who emigrated there prior to World War II. About 1950 Rothko achieved the mature style of which *Reds Number 5,* done nine years before his death, is a superb example.

Three red rectangles have been placed one above the other on a canvas stained with thin red paint. All three fields are of different size and their colour intensity varies; yet together they expand to fill almost the entire surface of the painting. The contours of these component fields are blurred and flowing, revealing strips of the ground between them and along their periphery. Thus rather than appearing solidly superimposed on the background the colour fields seem to oscillate, vibrating and pulsating at some indeterminate depth. And just as the fields are not clearly delineated, the picture plane as a whole seems to possess no sharp borders; it stands in a relationship of tension to the wall behind and around it and thus to the entire room.

This effect of existing actively in space draws the viewer inexorably into the image and lends the colours an almost physical presence. The three fields hover before our eyes like apparitions, inducing a meditative mood in which the translucent veils can be contemplated without the need to explain them rationally. The kind of experience which Rothko's painting offers might be called a metaphysical reaction to a reality created by the artist, the reality of the image, which Rothko himself once called "tragic and timeless." What Rothko's images give us is one of the most extreme possibilities ever achieved of experiencing reality through art.

MP

52 Frank Stella (b. 1936)

Sanbornville I, 1966.
Fluorescent alkyd and epoxy resin on canvas, 371 × 264 × 10 cm.

Together with Donald Judd, the principal representative of Minimal Art, and Elsworth Kelly, the first of the Hard Edge Abstractionists, Frank Stella ranks among the finest of those young American artists who pared the colour fields and existential gestures of Post-Painterly Abstraction down to more objective, sharper and precisely defined forms. Stella began with the all-over principle worked out by Jackson Pollock, where the painting surface is covered evenly with shapes and traces which do not congeal into configurations independent of the image as a whole. As early as his *Black Paintings* of 1958, he contained the energy of the gestural stroke in geometric forms which were so strongly identified with the picture plane that its borders were simultaneously the limits of the structure developed within it. The painting and its content became one. The image was only that and nothing more; it signalled a departure from traditional, illusionary painting.

This approach led Stella logically to the typical "shaped canvases" which he began in 1960. Here, he cut everything away from the rectangular periphery of the painting that was not defined by its internal forms.

The canvas in our collection belongs to the Irregular Polygon Series which Stella executed from spring 1965 to summer 1967. This sequence comprises a total of eleven different compositions bearing the names of towns in New Hampshire, each of which was done in four versions with different colour schemes (a variation on *Sanbornville I* now hangs in the Landesmuseum, Münster). Stella attempted in this series to overcome the two-dimensionality of the painted surface and relate the forms, developed out of equilateral triangles, to the surrounding space. The lapidary, uncompromising look of this conception is typical of the 1960s New York School.

DH

53 Francis Bacon (b. 1909)

Portrait of Isabel Rawsthorne standing in a Street in Soho, 1967.
Oil on canvas, 198 × 147 cm.

Bacon originates from Dublin. His parents gave him no support in his desire to become an artist, and so he worked as an interior designer until, in the late 1920s, he decided to paint full time. Largely self-taught, he had soon found the subject-matter that was to shape his life's work – human beings obsessed and deformed by anxiety.

News photographs of open-mouthed, self-satisfied political speakers inspired his imagery as much as stills from such films as Eisenstein's *Battleship Potemkin* (1925) and paintings of the past like Poussin's *Slaughter of the Innocents,* Rembrandt's evanescent self-portraits, Fuseli's haunting nightmares, van Gogh's portraits, and Picasso's Surrealist bathers. Bacon worked in series from the start, capturing one and the same model in changing attitudes, motion-studies sometimes integrated in one picture but more often spread over the three canvases of a triptych. He usually took photographs to work from, which gave him more liberty vis-à-vis his model, enabling him, as he once said, to recreate the person he wished to portray.

A photo of this kind exists of Isabel Lambert Rawsthorne, artist and wife of the composer Alan Rawsthorne. Bacon portrayed her over and over again from 1964 on. In addition to this full-length portrait the Nationalgalerie has a second painting of the same year in its collection, *Three Studies of Isabel Rawsthorne.* In this larger of the two paintings she has been depicted standing in a kind of revolving door, or a transparent cage, a motif which, like panes of glass, often appears in Bacon's work and can be interpreted as a symbol of modern man's isolation or imprisonment in self. Compared to other and particularly to later images, the figure here is still relatively undistorted and focussed. Portrait character has been retained, in spite of the dissolution of the figure especially in the area of extremities and face, a stripping-off of masks to lay bare that animal layer devoid of individuality and evocative of terror – terror because we recognize in it the aspect of our own humanity.

AS

List of plates

1 Gottlieb Schick (1776–1812)
Portrait of Heinrike Dannecker (1773–1823),
1802.
Oil on canvas, 119 × 100 cm
Inv. No. A II 840, NG 1762

2 Friedrich Overbeck (1789–1869)
The Painter Franz Pforr, c. 1810–12.
Oil on canvas, 62 × 47 cm
Inv. No. A II 381, NG 1002

3 Josef Anton Koch (1768–1839)
The Falls at Subiaco, 1813.
Oil on canvas, 58 × 68 cm
Inv. No. A I 407, NG 554

4, 5 Caspar David Friedrich
(1774–1840)
The Solitary Tree (Village Landscape
in Morning Light), 1822;
Moonrise over the Sea, 1822.
Both oil on canvas, 55 × 71 cm
Inv. Nos. NG 77 and NG 78

6 Karl Friedrich Schinkel (1781–1841)
Banks of the Spree near Stralau, 1817.
Oil on canvas, 36 × 44.5 cm
Inv. No. NG Wolzogen A 15

7 Eduard Gaertner (1801–1877)
Parochialstrasse (formerly Reetzengasse), 1831.
Oil on canvas, 39 × 29 cm
Inv. No. NG 81

8 Karl Blechen (1798–1840)
Interior of the Palm House, 1832.
Oil on paper mounted on canvas, 64 × 56 cm
Inv. No. A I 617

9 Karl Spitzweg (1808–1885)
The Poor Poet, 1839.
Oil on canvas, 36,3 × 44,7 cm
Inv. No. A I 1032, NG 1118

10 John Constable (1776–1837)
The Admiral's House in Hampstead, or
"The Grove", 1821–22.
Oil on canvas, 60 × 50 cm
Inv. No. A I 850, NG 889

11 Carl Rottmann (1797–1850)
Battlefield at Marathon, c. 1849.
Oil on canvas, 91 × 90.5 cm
Inv. No. A I 209, NG 282

12 Adolph von Menzel (1815–1905)
The Balcony Room, 1845.
Oil on cardboard, 58 × 47 cm
Inv. No. A I 1744, NG 845

13 Adolph von Menzel (1815–1905)
The Flute Concert, 1852.
Oil on canvas, 142 × 205 cm
Inv. No. A I 206, NG 219

14 Anselm Feuerbach (1829–1880)
Ricordo di Tivoli, 1866–67.
Oil on canvas, 194 × 131 cm
Inv. No. A I 732, NG 835

15 Hans von Marées (1837–1887)
The Rowers, 1873.
Oil on canvas, 136 × 167 cm
Inv. No. A I 1024, NG 1224

16 Hans von Marées (1837–1887)
The Golden Age (The Ages of Life), c. 1878.
Oil and tempera on panel, 98 × 87 cm
Inv. No. NG 960

17 Arnold Böcklin (1827–1901)
Self-portrait with Death as Fiddler, 1872.
Oil on canvas, 75 × 61 cm
Inv. No. A I 633, NG 772

18 Gustave Courbet (1819–1877)
The Wave (La Vague), 1870.
Oil on canvas, 112 × 144 cm
Inv. No. A I 967, NG 891

19 Wilhelm Leibl (1844–1900)
Dachau Woman with Child, 1873–74.
Oil on panel, 86 × 68 cm
Inv. No. A I 824, NG 947

20 Claude Monet (1840–1926)
St. Germain l'Auxerrois, 1866.
Oil on canvas, 79 × 98 cm
Inv. No. A I 984, NG 998

21 Claude Monet (1840–1926)
Summer, 1874.
Oil on canvas, 57 × 80 cm
Inv. No. A I 1013, NG 1146

22 Pierre Auguste Renoir (1841–1919)
Summertime, 1868.
Oil on canvas, 85 × 59 cm
Inv. No. A I 1019, NG 1073

23 Edouard Manet (1832–1883)
The Conservatory (Dans la serre), 1879.
Oil on canvas, 115 × 150 cm
Inv. No. A II 550, NG 693

24 Edouard Manet (1832–1883)
A Bunch of Lilacs, c. 1882.
Oil on canvas, 54 × 42 cm
Inv. No. A II 379, NG 1333

25 Max Liebermann (1847–1935)
The Stevenstift in Leyden, 1889.
Oil on canvas, 78 × 100 cm
Inv. No. FNG 1/78

26 Lovis Corinth (1858–1925)
Donna Gravida, 1909.
Oil on canvas, 95 × 79 cm
Inv. No. A II 143, NG 1262

27 Max Slevogt (1862–1932)
Still-life with Lemons, 1921.
Oil on canvas, 64 × 80 cm
Inv. No. A II 500, NG 1588

28 Edvard Munch (1863–1944)
Count Harry Kessler, 1906.
Oil on canvas, 200 × 84 cm
Inv. No. B 50, Gal. 20. Jh. No. 172

29 Oskar Kokoschka (1886–1980)
The Vienna Architect Adolf Loos, 1909.
Oil on canvas, 74 × 91 cm
Inv. No. A II 448, NG 1482

30 Emil Nolde (1867–1956)
Pentecost, 1909.
Oil on canvas, 87 × 107 cm
Inv. No. NG 7/74

31 Erich Heckel (1883–1970)
Landscape near Dresden, 1910.
Oil on canvas, 66.5 × 78.5 cm
Inv. No. B 30, Gal. 20. Jh. No. 83

32 Karl Schmidt-Rottluff (1884–1976)
Farmyard at Dangast, 1910.
Oil on canvas, 86.5 × 94.5 cm
Inv. No. B 86a, Gal. 20. Jh. No. 198

33 Ernst Ludwig Kirchner (1880–1938)
Belle Alliance Square, Berlin, 1914.
Oil on canvas, 96 × 85 cm
Inv. No. B 129, Gal. 20. Jh. No. 123

34 Vladimir Tatlin (1885–1953)
Composition, 1916.
Tempera, oil and gouache on panel, 52 × 39 cm
Inv. No. B 1100

35 George Grosz (1893–1959)
Pillars of Society, 1926.
Oil on canvas, 200 × 108 cm
Inv. No. NG 4/58

36 Otto Dix (1891–1961)
The Art Dealer Alfred Flechtheim, 1926.
Mixed media on panel, 120 × 80 cm
Inv. No. NG 46/61

37 Laszlo Moholy-Nagy (1895–1946)
Composition Z VIII, 1924.
Distemper on canvas, 114 × 132 cm
Inv. No. NG 5/59

38 Paul Klee (1879–1940)
The Ships' Departure, 1927.
Oil on canvas, 51 × 65.5 cm
Inv. No. NG 22/67

39 Giorgio de Chirico (1888–1979)
The Great Metaphysician, c. 1923–24.
Oil on canvas, 110 × 80 cm
Inv. No. B 770

40 René Magritte (1898–1967)
L'idée fixe, 1927.
Oil on canvas, 81 × 115 cm
Inv. No. 12/75

41 Max Ernst (1891–1976)
The Chosen Bride of Evil, 1928.
Oil on canvas, 198 × 303 cm
Inv. No. B 893

42 Fernand Léger (1881–1955)
The Two Sisters, 1935.
Oil on canvas, 162 × 114 cm
Inv. No. 3/79

43 Max Beckmann (1884–1950)
Death, 1938.
Oil on canvas, 121 × 176.5 cm
Inv. No. B 80, Gal. 20. Jh. No. 18

44 Giorgio Morandi (1890–1964)
Still-life with Bottles, 1940.
Oil on canvas, 47 × 52.8 cm
Inv. No. B 913

45 Karl (Carl) Hofer (1878–1955)
The Black Rooms, 1943.
Oil on canvas, 149 × 110 cm
Inv. No. B 2, Gal. 20. Jh. No. 100

46 Salvador Dali (b. 1904)
Mrs. Isabel Styler-Tas (Melancolia), 1945.
Oil on canvas, 65.5 × 86 cm
Inv. No. B 359, Gal. 20. Jh. No. 36

47 Wols (Alfred Otto Wolfgang Schulze) (1913–1951)
Painting, 1946–47.
Oil on canvas, 80 × 80 cm.
Inv. No. B 1042

48 Ernst Wilhelm Nay (1902–1968)
Mélisande, 1948.
Oil on canvas, 90 × 60 cm
Inv. No. B 236, Gal. 20. Jh. No. 178

49 Willi Baumeister (1889–1955)
Montaru 8, 1953.
Oil on hardboard, 130 × 100 cm
Inv. No. B 134, Gal. 20. Jh. No. 14

50 Serge Poliakoff (1906–1969)
Composition with Red and Yellow Shapes, 1963.
Oil on canvas, 157 × 127 cm
Inv. No. 28/68

51 Mark Rothko (1903–1970)
Reds Number 5, 1961.
Oil on canvas, 177.8 × 160 cm
Inv. No. B 896

52 Frank Stella (b. 1936)
Sanbornville I, 1966.
Fluorescent alkyd and epoxy resin on canvas,
371 × 264 × 10 cm
Inv. No. B 1063

53 Francis Bacon (b. 1909)
Portrait of Isabel Rawsthorne standing in a
Street in Soho, 1967.
Oil on canvas, 198 × 147 cm
Inv. No. B 897

Literature

Catalogues:

Kataloge der Gemäldesammlung des Joachim Heinrich Wilhelm Wagener von 1828 bis 1873
Verzeichnisse und Kataloge der Nationalgalerie von 1876 bis 1934
Lionel von Donop: Katalog der Handzeichnungen, Aquarelle und Ölstudien in der Königlichen National-Galerie, Berlin 1902
Hans Mackowsky: Führer durch die Bildnis-Sammlung, Berlin 1929
Paul Ortwin Rave: Das Rauch-Museum in der Orangerie des Charlottenburger Schlosses, Berlin 1930
Paul Ortwin Rave: Das Schinkel-Museum und die Kunst-Sammlungen Beuths, Berlin 1931
Die wichtigsten Erwerbungen in den Jahren 1933 bis 1937, Berlin 1938
Adolf Jannasch: Galerie des 20. Jahrhunderts, Berlin von 1953 bis 1962
Verzeichnis der Gemälde und Bildwerke der Nationalgalerie Berlin in der Orangerie des Schlosses Charlottenburg von 1961 bis 1966
Verzeichnis der Vereinigten Kunstsammlungen Nationalgalerie (Preußischer Kulturbesitz) / Galerie des 20. Jahrhunderts (Land Berlin), Berlin 1968
Neuerwerbungen der Nationalgalerie 1967—1972, Berlin 1972
Verzeichnis der Gemälde und Skulpturen des 19. Jahrhunderts, Nationalgalerie Berlin, Staatliche Museen Preußischer Kulturbesitz, Berlin 1976
Freunde danken Werner Haftmann. Ausstellung der Schenkungen an die Nationalgalerie, Berlin 1976
Deutsche Zeichnungen der klassischen Moderne aus der Nationalgalerie Berlin, Berlin 1976—77
Edward Kienholz: "Volksempfängers", Berlin 1977
Edvard Munch: Der Lebensfries für Max Reinhardts Kammerspiele, Berlin 1978

Nationalgalerie Berlin — 10 Jahre im neuen Haus, Bonn-Bad Godesberg/Berlin 1978—79
Kunst des 20. Jahrhunderts. Ein Führer durch die Sammlung, Berlin 1980
Prints and Drawings by Adolph Menzel. A selection from the collections of the museums of West Berlin, Berlin 1984

Publications:

Werner Haftmann: Die Neue Nationalgalerie. Staatliche Museen Preußischer Kulturbesitz, Berliner Forum 3/69, Berlin 1969
Alfred Hentzen: Die Berliner National-Galerie im Bildersturm. Berlin 1971
Dieter Honisch: Nationalgalerie Berlin, Recklinghausen 1979
Adolf Jannasch: Die Galerie des 20. Jahrhunderts Berlin 1945—1968, Berlin 1968
Christos Joachimides: Joseph Beuys. Richtkräfte, Nationalgalerie Berlin 1977
Ludwig Justi: Deutsche Malkunst im 19. Jahrhundert. Ein Führer durch die National-Galerie, Berlin 1920
Ludwig Justi: Die Ankäufe des Vereins "Freunde der National-Galarie", Berlin 1930
Ludwig Justi: Von Corinth bis Klee, Berlin 1931
Ludwig Justi: Von Runge bis Thoma, Berlin 1932
Ludwig Justi: Im Dienste der Kunst, Breslau 1936
Peter Krieger: Maler des Impressionismus. Bilderhefte der Staatlichen Museen, Berlin 1967
Paul Ortwin Rave: Die Malerei des 19. Jahrhunderts. 240 Bilder nach Gemälden der National-Galerie, Berlin 1945
Paul Ortwin Rave: Die Geschichte der Nationalgalerie Berlin, Berlin 1968
Karl Scheffler: Berliner Museumskrieg. Berlin 1921
Hugo von Tschudi: Gesammelte Schriften zur neueren Kunst, München 1912